"*Brave in Real Life* is a c...
ror and triumph. Each ta...
while exposing the insidious en...
prepared to have your heart pulled and your life empowered
to help prevent this tragedy."

—**LISA BEVERE**, NEW YORK TIMES
BESTSELLING AUTHOR

"*Brave in Real Life* digs its teeth into the raw underbelly of
evil and pulls everything out into the open. It's a powerful re-
minder that our past does not determine our future and that
redemption is possible for absolutely everyone."

—**PAUL BURNS**, *MANAGING DIRECTOR,*
TWITTER

"This book beautifully amplifies the voices of those we over-
look. Their stories resonate with heartbreak and courage.
Don't turn away. This message is too important."

—**CRAIG GREENFIELD**, *FOUNDER,*
ALONGSIDERS INTERNATIONAL;
AUTHOR, SUBVERSIVE JESUS

"*Brave in Real Life* will not only inspire you but has the potential to change your life. More than mere rhetoric about living
bravely, Guy Chevreau shares true stories of courage and hope
that desperately need to be told."

—**AMY GROESCHEL**, *CO-FOUNDER, LIFE. CHURCH,*
OKLAHOMA; AUTHOR; FOUNDER, BRANCH15

"*Brave in Real Life* is an excellent collection of human trafficking survivor stories, each one unique yet similar. There is no cookie-cutter playbook for human trafficking. Vulnerability is a common theme that I have seen in my experience with human trafficking victims.

I learned from the best: survivors. Written law, classrooms, and text books cannot make you understand the complexities of human trafficking. Listening to survivors' stories, and hearing their words and their experiences is essential to begin to understand."

—**SERGEANT BRAD BROOKER**,
KINGSTON CITY POLICE, ONTARIO

"*Brave in Real Life* is a deeply engaging book. I couldn't put it down. Guy has captured the voice of the women and conveyed their horrible trauma and abuse without salacious or distasteful detail. Threaded through each story line is hope and renewal—a hope that renews my own spirit as I prayerfully strive to be one of the 'small dots' that connect women to a life that overcomes."

—**CHARLOTTE PAONESSA**, *COURT CHAPLAIN, TORONTO*

"This collection of stories from women who experienced human trafficking is shocking and heartbreaking. With every page we're reminded that each of us is created in the image of God and that he is moving even in the darkest places. The best hope for breaking through this darkness comes through survivors courageously sharing their experience and redemption."

—**MICHAEL CHITWOOD**, *EXECUTIVE DIRECTOR FOR CHURCH AND MINISTRY PARTNERS, WORLD VISION U.S.*

Stories From Women Who Have Overcome Sexual Exploitation

BRAVE IN REAL LIFE

GUY CHEVREAU

10O
MOVEMENTS
PUBLISHING

BRAVE *Global*™

First published in 2021 by 100 Movements Publishing
www.100Mpublishing.com
Copyright © 2021 by Guy Chevreau and BRAVE Global

www.100Mpublishing.com
www.movementleaderscollective.com
www.catalysechange.org

ISBN 978-1-7355988-7-1 (paperback)
ISBN 978-1-955142-06-9 (ebook)

Editor in chief: Miley Waterman
Cover design: Tony Honkawa

100 Movements Publishing
An imprint of Movement Leaders Collective
Cody, Wyoming

If to be feeling alive to the sufferings of my fellow-creatures,
and to be warmed with the desire of relieving their
distresses, is to be a fanatic,
I am one of the most incurable fanatics ever
permitted to be at large.

William Wilberforce (1759–1833) on his commitment to
abolish the slave trade

Donations to BRAVE can be made as follows:

US
Visit braveglobal.org/donate for BRAVE Global's mailing address or to make an online donation.

Canada
Visit braveglobal.ca/donate for BRAVE Canada's mailing address or to make an online donation.

This book is dedicated
to those who feel they have no hope.

Brave [breyv]

adjective, **brav-er, brav-est.**
possessing or exhibiting courageous endurance;
confident fortitude that actively faces and endures
anything threatening

verb
to defy; challenge; dare

(of a person)
willing to do things that are difficult, dangerous
or painful; not afraid

CONTENTS

DIAMONDS II

a precious commodity,
infinite value in a crystalline form of pure carbon,
the most beautiful naturally occurring substance in the world.

but diamonds are not found, they are made
by a loving hand, shaped like redemption
to knock the dirt off its shoulders and
bring it to life.

they take strength to lift.
because jewels that are heavy with purpose
do not bounce.
not everyone will be able to hold on to something so precious.

there are millions of diamonds all over this world lying
undiscovered.
because it takes a master trained eye to see a diamond's worth.

a diamond is small, but it can cut through anything.
they can survive impact and still not be broken.
they can withstand temperature change
so, turn up the heat.

if each struggle is a gem in the crown i wear,
then each day crown me again.
how can i take these rough-cut pieces
and buff them to a brilliant shine?

no, i did not wake up like this.
i will never be flawless
but in the light of love i am blameless.
it chisels every ache into accolade.
every jagged angle into winged angel,
because God is Love,
and Love … it
turns coal into diamonds.

By Dagmar Morgan, used by gracious permission.

FOREWORD

It was in the middle of a brothel tour that I wondered it aloud. The operator and manager of two local brothels—let's call her Susan—was showing me around her latest renovations. She was proud of her work, and I was fumbling for words, trying to be supportive of *her* without endorsing the exploitation she was serving.

I knew Susan to be strong and confident, a no-nonsense, don't-mess-with-me, tell-it-like-it-is type of force—the kind of person you definitely do not want to tangle with. We had an unlikely friendship. We found ourselves at the opposite sides of the city's raging debate about how to tackle indoor prostitution—she was campaigning to legalize the sex industry, somehow hoping to legitimize her "work," and I was trying to shut it down to liberate her and those like her from their exploitation, whether they liked it or not! After some harsh debates, we would often meet for lunch to catch up. Somehow, who we were to each other mattered more than what we believed.

So, back to my fumbling wondering. After seeing the clearly beautiful and creative renovations that had transformed a den of iniquity into an illusion of paradise, I found myself asking aloud, "You are so amazing, strong, talented, business-savvy, and capable—why do you do *this* with your life?"

Both of us were a little surprised at the way my question both startled and unnerved us. Susan took me by the arm and led me to a back room where she quickly closed the door behind us. She could not afford to show any of her girls her real self; the cost would be too great for all of them to bear. But behind that closed door, on that terrible and beautiful day, she began to answer my question.

"When I was eleven years old, I had been sexually assaulted by my father for the last time. I finally escaped that hell and found myself walking down this street—the very same street my brothel is located on—with no one to help me and nowhere to go. That's when a man in a pickup truck pulled over and offered me a place to stay for the night in exchange for sex. I turned my first 'trick' that night, and I cried the whole time. And I kept crying. Night after night I cried until I finally stopped crying. It was then that I decided I would make the best with the life I had been given. So here I am. Doing the best I can."

Susan turned towards me, the tears welled in her eyes, pooling and starting to spill, the pain etched into her weary face, and she said, "I guess the question I have for you, Danielle, is where were you when I was eleven?"

And that was it. That was the question that broke like a tsunami.

Not because she was in some way different than the hundreds of other women I had met all over the world on street corners and brothels and massage parlors and strip clubs, but because she was so similar. Her story was not the exception; it was the rule. And that's what broke me. It wasn't the specialness or sadness of her situation—it was the sheer normality of it. It was like that one story cascaded into every story I had ever heard, and I began to hear all of them at the same time. Capable, strong, beautiful, smart, talented, gifted, and resilient women had been reduced to statistics at the justice level and meat at the market of the so-called sex "industry," the lucrative exploitation that is the slavery of our time.

That was the birth of the BRAVE movement in my heart. The way it took shape in real life is like a breadcrumb trail, left by God himself, until I met the formidable force that is Noemi Chavez and the Revive Church advocates who had started answering the exact question echoing in my soul, with an event for vulnerable girls in Long Beach, California. It was called BRAVE. I felt like God had given us a key that would unlock exploitation for a generation of vulnerable girls.

At that point in my life, I had already been trying to fight human trafficking for dozens of years. I was a chaplain to the indoor industry; I'd set up survivor ministries, safe houses, community awareness programs, justice advocacy, and street-based outreaches. I had run for freedom, walked for justice, flash-mobbed for liberation, campaigned politically to pass new protective legislation, preached to churches, spoken to parliaments and politicians, and inspired teenagers, and, well, everything I could think of to try and stop the bleeding. But this was the day I was undone. And here's why: because of the power of story. Every story—the real struggle behind the matrix of exploitation—is where the *light* will dissipate the darkness! The truth *will* set us free.

The statistics are alarming, the realities are unnerving, and the task is enormous. But the power to change—the sheer audacity to hope for things to move; the resilience of women who have stared down the barrel of abuse and neglect and abandonment and addiction and slavery and have risen above it; the strength of those who have defied the devil and have dared to fight back and share their experience and hope—that's where all the *power* is. And although loads of anti-trafficking propaganda might tell you that the victims of sex trafficking are voiceless, I beg to differ. They have voices, and they are some of the most powerful prophetic witnesses on the planet. They have broken me, changed me, challenged me, saved me, convicted me, motivated me, inspired me, rebuked me, awakened me, and rescued me again and again from apathy, indifference, hopelessness, fear and loneliness, and most of all from the temptation towards despair, because although you will hear the dissonance of painful truth, you will also hear the melody of overcoming power. *It's the strength of a survivor's story.* Trust me, it will change you.

And that's why I'm so honored that my good friend Guy Chevreau has compiled this book of stories. They are real. They are true. They are beautiful. They are strong. They are necessary to move us to be brave, not on *behalf* of women survivors of sex trafficking—but *with* them. Guy is a gifted writer who has impacted my own life with his previous work. And precisely because he is a *man* who is willing to use his power, privilege, and gifts on behalf of and beside women, he sets an example that I hope many millions of other men will follow. Guy is not the hero of this tale; he is highlighting the real heroes—the women!

Their lives *lead* us and *invite* us to walk arm in arm together until this modern evil is banished. It will require much from us. These stories are brutal and vulnerable. They are honest and deep. And they will cause you to ache and to cry and to weep ... and that's okay. Actually, it's necessary. For the kind of movement we need to battle against the evil of sex trafficking will require an undoing—a terrible, beautiful day of reckoning—where the truth embraced and expressed becomes the starting place of transformation for all of us.

Let these mighty women who are the bravest I know lead you to join the story of brave in real life! Let the truth set us all free—together.

Danielle Strickland, co-founder of BRAVE Global
daniellestrickland.com

INTRODUCTION

My wife, Kerry, and I have a bookcase in our guest bedroom, and when we have overnight visitors we've come to expect the conversation that awaits us at breakfast. It won't be about Kerry's books on triathlon training.

Our guests wonder about the other books on the shelves, titles such as *Sex for Sale*; *Pimp Nation*; *Prostitution Narratives*; *Paying for Pleasure*; *Female Sexual Slavery*; *Gender and Justice*; *The Rich Get Richer and the Poor Get Prison*. Kerry explains that she recently completed a Master's in Criminology and Criminal Justice. Her thesis was titled, "Public Perceptions of Adult Prostitution in the UK." Our guests then typically ask why Kerry got into "all of that." If they're really interested, she serves them the whole enchilada.

For over ten years, Kerry worked professionally with vulnerable and at-risk youth. In 2012 she took a sabbatical and traveled to Thailand, where it is estimated that thirty-five thousand young girls and women are currently exploited in the sex industry. For six months Kerry volunteered at the Tamar Center in Pattaya. Their mandate was simple: offer a different way of life to anyone interested.

Kerry's time in Thailand left an indelible imprint on her heart and spirit, but on her return to the UK she wasn't sure what to do with the sense of call that she felt. Two years later, she and I attended the New Wine summer conference in the southwest of England. A Salvation Army officer named Danielle Strickland was one of the keynote speakers, and she held us spellbound as she told stories of her fight against human trafficking. While Danielle was speaking, Kerry had an unsettling sense that God was asking her to do a Master's in Criminology. That seemed logical; when she had interviewed for government anti-human trafficking positions, she continuously lost out to retired police officers. She concluded that a Master's in Criminology would help bridge a perceived gap in her résumé.

If our overnight guests are still interested, it's my turn to take over the story because I was also one of the speakers at that same New Wine conference. During a break in the program, Kerry and I met Danielle and her family. Danielle and her husband, Stephen, had read several of my books, and with lots to talk about, we had a very engaging lunch together.

A year later, Kerry and I moved from England to Toronto, and co-incidentally, Danielle and her family moved from Long Beach, California—also to Toronto. Several months after we were settled, Danielle and Stephen invited us to dinner. We talked at length about BRAVE, a new initiative Danielle was launching alongside her friends Noemi Chavez and Miley Waterman. Danielle, Noemi, Miley, and some of their colleagues were staggered to learn that a disproportionate number of girls who end up on the streets in the sex industry are from the foster care system. In 2013, 60 percent of child trafficking victims recovered through FBI raids in over seventy cites nationwide had histories in the child welfare system, and it's a percentage that continues to rise.[1] Although many are exploited against their will, it is not by coincidence that the majority of these girls end up selling themselves. They've been targeted and groomed with explicit purpose. BRAVE's mandate is a simple one: if those exploiting these girls can target them, why can't the church? God's people could reach out to vulnerable girls with a message of hope and empowerment— and do so before the pimps get to them.

■ ■ ■

In 1999 I wrote a book titled *We Dance Because We Cannot Fly: Stories of Redemption from Heroin to Hope.* The substance of the book came from the three months I spent living in a number of Betel communities across Europe. Betel is an organization that cares for recovering heroin addicts, and a number of men and women in their communities allowed me to interview them and tell their story, from the desperate bottoms of addiction to the restoration they've experienced through the power of God's love. It was one of my books that Danielle and Stephen had read.

While Kerry was doing her Master's work, I read many of the books she was using in her research. Characteristically, they were stories of survival, such as Rachel Moran's memoir *Paid For: My Journey Through Prostitution.*[2] I asked Danielle if anybody was writing a book about BRAVE stories ... because what characterized the stories that Danielle was telling was not just that women endured and survived horrific pasts, but that they *overcame*. I wondered if a book like *We Dance Because We Cannot Fly* might serve to inspire and encourage.

A year later, 2018, Kerry was working both as Danielle's executive assistant and as director of BRAVE Canada. I was asked to serve on the board of directors of BRAVE Canada, and over the past year, Kerry, Danielle, and others have referred me to various articles about human trafficking. I've also done my own research. It's made for some very disturbing reading. For instance:

"The epidemic of gender violence kills and disables more women and girls between the ages of 15 and 44 than cancer, traffic accidents, malaria, and war *combined*."[3]

"Globally, it's estimated that 1 in 3 women will experience physical or sexual abuse in their lifetime."[4]

"More than 1 in 3 women (35.6%) in the United States have experienced rape, physical violence, and/or stalking by an intimate partner in their lifetime."[5]

These statistics seemed unbelievable, until I read the following correlation:

> Sexual violence … is not only an epidemic—but it is also a *business*. That is to say, there is actually money to be made off rape and sexual assault—*a lot* of money.
> … It is a very untidy thought to realize that there is actually a vast business of rape for profit in the world.[6]

A quick google later, I was staggered to discover just how vast a business "rape for profit" actually is. In 2014, the International Labor Organization conservatively estimated that 4.8 million women were sexually exploited, and that exploitation generated ninety-nine *billion* dollars worldwide.[7]

There were other misconceptions that needed correcting. In my sheltered naïveté, I had thought that the sex trade was localized in places like Amsterdam and Southeast Asia and the red-light districts of major cities. Not so. In an article in *Fortune,* the chair of the Human Trafficking Advisory Council, Cindy McCain, states: "[Trafficking] is something that is hiding in plain sight. It's everywhere—it's absolutely everywhere."[8] This was echoed in a statement made by Toronto police Detective David Correa, of the Sex Crimes Human

Trafficking Enforcement Team: "Your postal code won't save you ... it doesn't shield you from the horrors of this type of exploitation."[9] Those at Covenant House Toronto, Canada's largest homeless youth agency, make this unsettling reality even more explicit:

> Anyone can become a victim of human trafficking. ... In recent years, individuals with relatively stable backgrounds are increasingly becoming victims of human trafficking. Victims who are trafficked by individuals under the age of 18 years are usually under 18 years old themselves. ... Homeless youth are among the most vulnerable to exploitation; however unsuspecting girls are also ensnared online, in malls and in school yards. ... Trafficking victims can come from any neighbourhood.[10]

■ ■ ■

I've been asked the question: "Why is a man telling these stories?" My answer is simple. I believe that redemption is not gender-specific. This book gives voice to those who were forced to keep silent for so long, and it is hoped that my contributions help heal, not just the wounds of those who tell their stories, but those whose secrets still torment, and distort, and steal.

The stories that follow are transcribed and edited interviews that I conducted, and each of the women you will meet chapter by chapter are remarkable on so many counts. To listen to them—as they have told of what they have endured, what they have survived, and what they have overcome—has been a tremendous privilege, and I thank each one of them for trusting me as quickly and deeply as they have.

The stories contained within these pages are profoundly emotive, and for that reason you may choose to pause between each account. At the end of each chapter we've intentionally included a blank page, which might be gratefully received as a chance to catch your breath, to attend to what's been stirred within your heart, and provide space to capture a quote, or to scribble some personal reflections before moving on to the next chapter.

It's also important to clarify that each of these women not only has a unique story, but a unique "voice." Their grammatical constructions and vocabulary are similarly unique, and so when you hit a sentence that may perhaps read a little "rough," remind yourself that these are real women who have lived on the rough side of life. So rough, many of them switched to telling their story in the present tense—so profound was the trauma they endured.

The stories gathered together in this book are like snapshots—true in the moment they were taken. We are all on a journey; we are all in process. As they share their stories with you, hold them in your thoughts and prayers, and believe for even further healing from the traumas they've endured.

■ ■ ■

In putting this book together, I've drawn inspiration from a statement made by the founder and president of International Justice Mission, Gary Haugen.[11] He states that historically, movements of reform were frequently given critical initial momentum from extraordinary journalists, preachers, reformers, academics, investigators, lawyers, politicians, and rabble-rousers who suddenly flipped on the lights to expose what had been hiding in the shadows ... they took the truth that everybody knew ... and made it a truth no one could ignore.[12]

It is our hope and prayer that *Brave in Real Life* helps to flip on the lights.

1

O ROMEO, ROMEO!
WHEREFORE ART
THOU ROMEO?

It's a ratio. It's a mathematical formula and you express it
in the form of a fraction and the way it works is this: the
number on top you want to be as high as possible. You
want a woman who's the most attractive you can find. That's
the top half of the equation. Bottom half of the equation?
The lowest possible self-esteem. And that produces a ratio.
The higher the ratio, the more you should go for it.[1]

TOM LEYKIS

Dear, sweet Juliet: Romeo may be a lot closer than you think. And he may not be the man you hope he is. Sure, he's told you he loves you. That he *really* loves you. Yes, he has been so kind to you, lavishing all sorts of gifts upon you—a new phone, clothes, shoes. And yes, he tells you all the time how crazy he is about you, that he can't stop thinking about you when you're apart.

Don't be surprised when he says he'd really like some pictures of you. He wants to be able to look at you when he's not with you. Your new phone takes great pics—how about dressing really sexy for him and taking a few selfies? You're *so* gorgeous...

He's big into the party scene, and yes, Juliet, the way he shows you off to his friends is a thrill. But one afternoon soon, he'll text to say that he has to work late and won't be able to pick you up. He's arranged for an Uber to take you to the party. He'll meet you there. Little do you know that the party is at a rented Airbnb, so no one will ever know where you were or how you got there.

This is a special party because he's going to show you off to his friends in a whole new way. He'll call it "sexual favors" for some of his buddies. You'll protest; you're a good girl, and you're not into that kind of party. He'll take you aside and remind you of the photos he has on his phone. Then he'll ask, "Want Mommy and Daddy to see what their little girl looks like now?"

It's called "iPhone blackmail," sweetheart. And Romeo has just changed your future. He'll be advertising you on Craigslist and selling you by the hour. You'll be moving a lot because he'll be following the "ten-day rule." He'll keep you in a different hotel room so that no one will ever find you.

■ ■ ■

As of January 2011, the majority of Canadian sex trafficking cases before the courts involved "trafficker-boyfriends." Their tactics are commonly referred to as "Romeo recruitment."[2] But this is not only a Canadian phenomenon. Sharon Marcus-Kurn, an assistant US attorney for the district of Columbia stated, "I've never met a juvenile in prostitution who hasn't said during the initial interview, 'I don't have a pimp—that guy is my boyfriend.'"[3]

The average age of those trafficked is thirteen to fourteen years old. There's a simple reason they're so young. Younger victims are easier to manipulate and control, and social media makes for easy pickings. When a girl posts online that she broke up with her boyfriend, or that she's always fighting with her father, or that she's run away and has no money, the pimps have hit a gold mine.

One girl explained that she and her Romeo had been texting back and forth for months. She said, "Usually, I know it's not true, but I thought I was going to live a love story." Within weeks, she was confined to an apartment and forced to service seven to ten men every night— and hand her "wages" over to her "boyfriend."[4]

On average, an underage girl will see ten clients a night. Some see as many as twenty.[5] Each visit will last about a half hour, and will cost between $100–200. She may well work seven nights a week. The math is staggering: $100 per client, ten clients per night—yields $1,000. At five nights a week, she's earning $250,000 a year.[6] And that's a conservative estimate. In 2010, the Criminal Intelligence Service Canada estimated that domestic sex traffickers generate an average of $280,000 annually from every victim under their control.[7] This is a trade that far exceeds profits from the sale of illegal drugs. In an interview with Sergeant Brad Brooker, Kingston City Police, I asked if that was indeed true. He assured me it was and offered this explanation: "A girl can be sold over and over again. A kilo of cocaine only gets sold once."[8]

■ ■ ■

What Romeo has promised his girl is that they're "working together towards a better life." Her Romeo boyfriend will feed her. He'll buy her clothes, and while he's "dating" her, he'll be pushing her sexual boundaries. It won't be long before he takes away her phone. Then she'll be doing favors. And once she's put out to work, she'll be forced to hand over all of the money she earns. And Romeo may well have several "girlfriends" working in the same hotel, at the same time.

A mental or emotional breakdown, or drug addiction, or a combination of the three will often render a girl unusable within two to five years. She will be abandoned by her Romeo—literally dumped in a back-alley of an urban center, and, as a completely broken human being, she will be left to fend for herself. Romeo will move on, at least a million dollars richer.

> "Romeo, the love I bear thee can afford
> No better term than this:
> thou art a villain."[9]

■ ■ ■

Mariah didn't fall in love with Romeo. She thought the man who came into her life was her Prince Charming. But there's not much in a name. He was no less a villain than Romeo.

When Mariah was eighteen years old, her mom was at risk of ovarian cancer. A surgeon cut out her mother's ovaries and uterus. There were then serious complications, and after the surgery her mother went into septic shock and very nearly died. All her vital organs were shutting down. After three months on life-support, another doctor finally figured out what was wrong, and he saved her life.

The surgery and the subsequent complications weren't the only things that weighed on Mariah's mind. Growing up, her dad was an absent father. Mariah called the one man in her life "Uncle." When Mariah was seven, "Uncle" started to sexually abuse her. The discovery of what became a year-long molestation had such a devastating effect on her mother's mental health that her mother spiraled into an uncontrollable manic depression. She was so drugged up on different medications, she never really left her bedroom. Mariah grew up as the primary caretaker of the family, and she didn't have an easy time of it.

■ ■ ■

'D GROWN UP AS A welfare baby. When I turned eighteen, we no longer got any income from the State. During my mom's time in hospital, our church had helped us out with our rent and kindly allowed us to get first pick of the food drives every second Saturday of the month. But they were only able to do that for a couple months. When that stopped, we couldn't pay our rent or electricity, or any other bills that began to add up.

One day I was walking my dog, and I met a guy who seemed like he was my Prince Charming. This gentleman could see that I was struggling. He knew I was upset. He asked what was wrong, and I told him about how sick my mom was, and how we couldn't pay the rent. He told me that a pretty girl shouldn't look so sad; he'd like to get to know me, and see if he could help. His name was Hamadi.[10]

Over the next few weeks I met him a couple of times, and he became my boyfriend, even though he was twelve years older than me. He became my Superman, my protector. He saved me from constant physical abuse from my brother. He put food in the house. The day he met my mom, he brought her flowers. He'd take me to get my nails done. He would take me out. He would buy me things. I liked the fact that he wanted to be with me all the time. I never thought it was because he didn't want to let me out of his sight.

On my nineteenth birthday he said, 'I'm going to take you to a club.' And I was thinking, like a nightclub or something.

We got there, and it's a strip club. Within five minutes of us sitting down, four or five girls were at our table. They laid all of their money out in front of me, and they're trying to convince me to dance that night. The owner came by and paid me all these compliments, saying he liked the way I walked, the way I carried myself. He said I had very expensive sex appeal. He tried to get me up dancing that night too.

I didn't dance that night, so all the way home Hamadi kept telling me, 'You can't afford the rent. You guys are getting another eviction notice. What are you going to do? You need to figure out how to make some money.'

That was during the time our church was helping us a lot, but I knew they could only do it for so long. It was so stressful. I could live with no food, but I couldn't live with no roof over my head.

One night we were drinking, and Hamadi finally convinced me to dance—just once. He bought me some heels, took me to a club, and I came home with $800. After that, he kept putting me out there every night, saying, 'We gotta put money to the bills.' I just kept giving him my money because he was assuring me, 'We're going to pay your mom's rent.'

After a couple of weeks went by, I said, 'Hey, I really need to pay her rent.'

When I said that, he snapped. He was already pissed because I'd become friends with one of the girls in the club, and he didn't want me to have any other friends but him. He was screaming so loud and driving so fast. It really scared me. I was thinking, *When I get home, I'm going to jump out of his car and run. He can keep everything—all the money I've earned. I need to get clear of him. I'll get ahead of him, and I'll slam the security gate shut.* The security gate to our building had metal rods sticking out of the top of it. You couldn't hop it unless you wanted those rods to go through you.

I managed to slam the gate on him, and I ran inside. Two weeks went by, and I hadn't seen or heard from him. I thought everything was good and everything was clear. I was hanging out with my brother, and my mom called me and said, 'You better get home right now. Your boyfriend is in here crying. How dare you ignore his phone calls? He's trying to get in contact with you. He's been nothing but a good man to you. He's taken care of you. He's taken care of this house.'

I knew I couldn't tell my mom what he was really like because I knew that if I told her the whole story it would put her into even more of a depression. I just told her, 'I'm not going to come home. I'm not talking to him, and he needs to get out of the house. Please kick him out. I will never come home if he's there.'

She wouldn't listen to me.

■ ■ ■

With no Hamadi around, the fights with my brother just got worse and worse. He shattered my elbow and busted up my face. It didn't help that my mom would tell me that if I didn't have such a smart-ass mouth I wouldn't get hit. It got so bad that I convinced myself anything would be better than living at home. I had to leave, and I couldn't go back with Hamadi because I knew that life was only going to get worse with him.

I posted a Facebook status that said, 'Looking for a room to rent.' I thought, *I can rent a room near the club, and pay my mom's rent from afar. I wouldn't have to pay anybody else, and*

I could just dance a couple of nights a week and cover all our bills.

A guy named Tyler[11] had been messaging me back and forth for some time. He texted and said, 'I have a room for rent. I know you don't have a car, so I can come get you and your things, and I'll take you to the place.' He sounded so sweet. He sounded so kind.

I should've known it was too good to be true. But instead of seeing red flags, I saw a way out.

I needed to make a complete break from Prince Charming and my toxic home life, so I was like, 'Yeah, sure.'

He came and picked me up and dropped me off at the place. It was a vacant motel with yellow *Caution* tape wrapped around it. They call it a 'trap house.' It's a very, very hidden, dirty apartment block where they conduct illegal activity. So it's guns, girls, drugs. There's no furniture. There's no electricity. It's just a hidden location that stays off the radar.

As I entered this apartment, I thought to myself, *What in hell did I get myself into?* But I needed a place to go. Tyler could tell I was desperate. He would hold me, and sweet-talk me. He was very romantic in a time of need. He got me settled in, on an air mattress. There was nothing else in the room. And then he left. I was there for two days on my own. My phone had died. I had no idea where I was at all. All I knew was it was almost a two-hour drive from Long Beach. It was definitely *not* a good place to be, and I knew I had to get out. Though there were chains on the front gates, I managed to find an exit route through a grimy stairwell leading to the back alley.

I started walking and came across an outdoor mall area that had a T-Mobile kiosk. They let me sign into my Gmail, and I got one of my friend's numbers from my address book, and I pleaded with him to come get me. The shop owner explained where we were, and my friend drove all the way out to get me.

When we got back to my mom's house, Tyler was outside of my apartment building. I hadn't noticed him sitting in his car across the way.

My friend dropped me off, and as I was walking up to my building, Tyler stepped out of his car and said, 'What are you doing?'

I looked up to see who was talking to me. Stunned, I said, 'I need clothes. You didn't come back, and I had no idea where I was.'

He said, 'Get back in the car. Let's go.'

I asked him, 'Can't I just go grab some clothes? I don't have anything to dance in.'

He's like, 'Okay, all right, let's go in.'

So I opened the gate, and he's right behind me. I can't slam the security gate behind me quick enough to keep him outside. At this point I was thinking if I can just get to our apartment, all I need is for somebody to be home, and I can tell them I don't want to leave. But my brother wasn't home. His girlfriend wasn't home. My mom wasn't home. No one was home.

There wasn't anybody there for me.

I got back in the car with Tyler, and he told me that I was in big trouble. I'd ruined the location of the trap house. He told me that he'd have to move me. We went back to the first place, and he said, 'Sit down and keep your head down. Don't talk to anybody.' He threw my stuff in a trash bag, and grabbed me and pulled me to my feet. 'Keep your head down, and don't talk.'

As I was walking out, another girl's walking in with her head down. We walked right past each other. She had her trash bag of stuff, and I had mine. I had to get in the car that she got out of. Tyler got in the back seat. They moved me to a whole other trap location that had a little patio, but it was all fenced in with bamboo sticks and chicken wire. There was no way you could get out.

Pimps line the whole hallway. I swear, every apartment in the building had to have a pimp. I was there for about four weeks. I hardly saw Tyler. He would come back every once in a while, but he really didn't have anything to do with me. He would just come back and say, 'You're doing good. You're doing good.' It didn't make any sense. All I was doing was just sitting there.

Tyler's 'roommate' would come by about every three days and ask, 'He hasn't put you to work yet? Has he fed you anything? Why doesn't he come and feed you? I can't let you go, so I guess I've got to feed you.'

Then he started taking me to a club without Tyler knowing about it. He would wait outside while I danced. After doing that a couple times he said, 'You owe me more money than what you're making, and he's not feeding you. I'm having to buy you food. I'm paying for the apartment.' Then he said, 'My cousin Liam[12] lives out in Vegas, and it's his birthday. I owe him a couple of favors, and you're going to be his birthday present. Don't worry—you'll have a better lifestyle out there.'

Tyler let me talk to Liam on the phone, and he told me I'd be living with him in his penthouse—no casinos or hotels. He said I'd be living like a star.

■ ■ ■

I didn't put up a fight. I couldn't go home; Prince Charming was still looking for me. There's nothing in LA for me. Tyler booked our tickets and traveled with me on the plane, and delivered me at the birthday party. He was right. Vegas was a better lifestyle. I was living in the penthouse—but I was never allowed out of Liam's sight. Ever. I couldn't even pee by myself. He was always right beside me.

The day of his birthday party, it was made clear what was going on and who was in charge. Liam drove me around from one casino to the next. Each stop, we picked up all his girls, one by one. We had to look our best as he paraded us around in the club he rented out for his birthday. It didn't take long to figure out who was his favorite. Ali was his top girl. She had his favor, and I knew if I did what she did, I would gain his favor too. I also learned what would happen if I didn't.

Later that night Ali came into the women's bathroom looking for me and a few of the other girls. I quickly followed her out. One girl remained behind, smoking a cigarette. She followed a minute later. I could see that Liam was not happy. We followed him out to the car for a 'team meeting.' He put me in the front seat. That had been Ali's seat. He began to talk about disrespect. He said that I was the new girl, and I showed him more respect than they did. And Ali was the head girl; she followed his instructions. One of those instructions was to go get us out of the bathroom and come to him immediately. He began to talk about the cigarette issue and how the girl didn't come right away. She went to say something, and he reached back and started beating her. He hit her harder and harder, telling her how I was a better example of staying in pocket than she was. Then he looked at me and said, 'Good girl.'

He dropped the girl he beat up at a casino hotel, and then returned to his party where he paraded the rest of us around. I knew I had to get home, but how?

It made me think of my mom's story. When she was thirteen she had been kidnapped by a pimp. My grandmother used to sell drugs to him, and over time the guy became infatuated with my mom, and he kidnapped her. I asked my mom, 'How did you make it out of there? What did you do while he was raping you?'

She said, 'I just let him believe his own fantasy.'

In my head I was like, *Okay, you know what? I'm just going to have to let Liam believe his own fantasy. You want me to call you 'Daddy'? Okay, Daddy. You want me to sit up straight? Okay. You want me to be your little money-maker? I'll be your little money-maker. Whatever you want.*

I just told him, 'I'll do whatever you want. Just don't put me on the track. I don't want to be out there prostituting. Just put me in the strip club. I promise I'll make the quota.'

I kept befriending him and letting him hear what he wanted to hear. I could tell he was starting to grow feelings for me. One thing led to another. He started to trust me. He let me text my mom and tell her that I was okay. One day he let me accept her phone call. She had called to tell me that she was going into an emergency surgery. I don't know if it was me hearing her voice, but the minute she said, 'Hey,' I just started crying, just utterly, ugly crying.

I knew she knew something was wrong because she knew all the signs of sex trafficking. She worked with Gems Uncovered[13] from the ground up. She had been in all the training. She worked with girls who'd been trafficked. She knew that was happening to me, but I didn't know how my mom was handling it. I just remember before I left, I took all of her pills, and I hid them at my neighbor's house because I knew Mom would try a suicide attempt if she really knew all I had been going through.

Liam was watching me bawling, and while I was still talking to my mom, he came over and was holding me and asking me, 'Are you okay, Baby? Everything okay?' He was believing his own fantasies. He believed he was this great lover and that I was now his top girl. He believed that I thought he was the one that could walk on water, that he was my everything.

I told him the situation, that my mom needed emergency surgery, but that she was refusing to do it 'til she had her kids by her side.

And he said, 'We'll get you a plane ticket. You're not staying at your family's house, though; me and you are going together. We're going for one day. You can see her before the surgery. You can see your mother after the surgery. But we're leaving later that night.'

He bought our plane tickets, and later that night he was taking me to work. We got pulled over by the police, and as we're pulling over he got on his phone real quick and then hung up. The police came up to talk to him, took his license and registration, and they went back to their patrol car. While they're running his information, another car pulls up in front of our car, and I was told to get into the car that had just pulled up. It was his cousin, and he drove me to the club and waited there for me while I danced my shift.

After work, he took me back to the house. I got a call from jail, and Liam said, 'I have a warrant for my arrest in Texas that I have to handle.'

I said, 'What about going to see my mom? I can go by myself. You can trust me. You're my everything. We're going to be the top of the empire; we're going to build, build, build. I'll never leave you. We're a good team.'

I fed him enough of his fantasy that he believed me.

He said I could fly out to see my mom by myself, but that there'd be somebody meeting me at the arrivals gate. He'd already arranged it with Tyler out in LA—the same guy that gave me away as a birthday present. He would take me to see my mom and then take me to the airport and put me on a plane back to Vegas.

Then he said, 'You're not allowed to take anything. Leave your social security card here. Take your travel ID, but nothing else. No luggage, nothing.'

That's what I did. I left Vegas with my travel ID and the clothes on my back. I don't know if Tyler was late or if my plane landed early, but I got off the plane, and no one was at my gate. I didn't have a phone, so I went up to the customer service desk, and I called my brother and told him I was at LAX. He drove over with his friend, and they picked me up and took me home.

■ ■ ■

Guys kept showing up at our security gate asking for me; I got all sorts of messages on Facebook and Instagram—scary stuff: 'You may have come back home. Don't worry, I'll come get you. I *will* find you.' There were times that I was followed … it was a very dangerous time in my life. But I had to pay the bills … so … I went back to dancing.

I had learned who to talk to and who not to talk to, and I stayed in one club. I had a good relationship with the manager.

Guys from the past would come to the club looking for me, and all I would have to do was tell my manager, 'He can't be in the club. He's dangerous for me,' and the bouncer would kick him out.

During that whole time, I felt like I was breathing under water because it was like God had me in this bubble of protection. Time and again the girls around me got beaten up because they smoked a cigarette or showed some attitude. I think the big difference was I was trying to play the game better than they were.

One year later, I met the man who became my husband. At that time, he was running a clothing business and asked me, if he gave me a job, would I quit dancing? I agreed, and together we worked on his business and took it to the top. We had so many orders we couldn't keep up with them all.

■ ■ ■

For the next three years, I was in denial—like nothing had ever happened. Why dwell on it? Just put it in the past. When memories did come back, I felt like it was my fault. I blamed myself about everything that happened. I was the one who put myself out there.

Soon after, I met Mary White. She is the founder of Gems Uncovered, and as a volunteer with Gems, my mom knew her really well. Mary would come up to me and say, 'Whenever you're ready, Mariah.' I didn't understand what she was saying or hinting at, but she would just say, 'Whenever you're ready, Mariah. All the glory be to God.' It didn't ever really click for me.

Our clothing business crashed after a bad business deal, so I took a job caregiving. I had a love-hate relationship with my job. I was a caretaker for the terminally ill, and I loved that part of my work. But the person I was taking care of had a son who was very mean to her. He was toxic around his mom, and it was a hard thing for me to see. That part of the job I hated, so much so that I only kept doing it because I needed to pay our bills.

It just became too much, and I was driving home from work one night, and my normal way home had got shut down 'cause they were working on the street. So I made a right. And then I made a left, and I dead-ended into another street. I pulled over, and all of a sudden, I could feel God's overwhelming presence. I started to cry, and I sensed that God said, 'Look up; look up, my child.' It was pouring down rain, so I could hardly see outside my windows. Through the flapping of the windshield wipers I could see a house in front of me, and it had a huge sign on it that said, 'All the glory be to God.' I could hear Mary White's voice in those words—it was exactly what she used to say—'All the glory be to God.'

I got out my phone, and I called her and said, 'I'm so sorry for being such an idiot. I'll come to the center. Can I come to the center?'

She said, 'What's going on? What's going on?'

I said, 'I'm sorry. I wasn't listening to you; I wasn't hearing you. I should have been listening, but I just wanted to run from it all. I didn't want to deal with it.'

She said what she's always said, 'Well, Mariah, whenever you're ready.' Then she asked, 'Where are you?'

I said, 'I'm in front of this house that has a huge sign in the window that says, 'All the glory be to God.'

She asked what street it was on. I told her, and she said, 'Mariah, that's our new home for the girls we're working with.'

Over the next months, Mary became my mentor. I started regular counseling and began resolving my issues. I had to deal with my daddy issues, and the fact that all of this mess wasn't my fault. I had run from it for so long—because I felt like it was a skeleton in my closet. I felt that it made people look at me like I caused all this, and I should own up to it.

■ ■ ■

I quit my job as a terminally-ill caretaker, and within a week I received a job offer from Helpline Youth Counseling to become a case manager for sex trafficking victims. These are hard girls to work with. It's not like these girls volunteer to be involved in the program or to work with me one-on-one. They came to me because they got caught by the police in sting operations, and most of them would not give up their traffickers' names because they were so caught up in the mental game and the manipulations. The girls were only there because the courts offered them these classes and the training, in lieu of arrest and criminal charges.

When you have someone speaking to you, and they don't know anything about human trafficking from the inside, it's different. They're teaching statistics and theories. They don't know what it is to live the lifestyle. If there's going to be significant change, they don't know all that has to be overcome. Though the girls didn't relate to a professional educator, they did to me. I wasn't speaking to the girls from an educator's point of view; I was speaking from a personal point of view, from first-hand experience. That got the girls' attention, and I was able to help them graduate the program, and then get back to school and start a new life. I was able to help more girls in one year than they had previously done in the last three years.

I worked with Helpline Youth Counseling for about a year, and because they're a huge non-profit organization, they paid for all my training. That gave me the qualifications I needed, and I was soon speaking in front of the Los Angeles Human Trafficking Task Force and leading training sessions with CIA agents.

And because I accomplished such a good turnaround with so many girls, the city asked Mary White if they could apply for grant money to move me across to work for Gems, so I could help with their programs.

■ ■ ■

I can't believe how far God has brought me. I had a crazy moment on Mother's Day this past year. My husband had bought me a new car, and when we were at the dealership picking it up, Hamadi—Prince Charming—was there with another girl. Years back, when I was with him, he'd taken me to a dealership and was stringing me the line: 'Look, we'll save up and get you a car like this.' I knew he was doing the same thing with that girl.

When he saw me, it was like he had seen a ghost. He grabbed the girl, and they left immediately. I just knew my presence shook him to the core. There I was, with my husband and my little boy. I have a life. I have a loving family. I have a future. And he had plans to steal all of that from the girl he was grooming.

IT'S EASIER TO COMPLY
THAN TO FIGHT

Homelessness is a recognized entry route into prostitution, which, in the case of young people and children, is often a result of running away. Running away can be an attempt to make a positive move, a means of breaking away from an intolerable home life in order to make a fresh start. It can also be seen as an attempt to exercise control over the situation. However, while a young woman may be making an attempt to be assertive, she would simultaneously be increasing her vulnerability to manipulation.[1]

BRITISH HOME OFFICE REPORT

Homelessness is so thoroughly and relentlessly traumatic a person will take any route, however dangerous or disgusting, to escape it.[2]

RACHEL MORAN, SURVIVOR

Growing up, I felt lonely, powerless and unloved. I made decisions that seemed harmless but, in fact, were very dangerous. … I wasn't foolish; I was vulnerable, naïve and a perfect target.[3]

CASANDRA DIAMOND, SURVIVOR

In June of 2019, after an absence of fifteen years, Alicia returned to her family home on the east coast of Canada. She had two reasons for making the trip. The first was that her elderly grandmother's health was declining, and she wanted to see her one last time. The second was that she wanted to make peace with the years she had spent there.

■ ■ ■

I DROPPED MY STUFF IN my old bedroom, and Mom went to work, just like she always did. I wandered around the house on my own. The stuff that had changed felt weird, but the stuff that hadn't changed felt weirder. At one point I went down the stairs, and on both sides of the walls were the family pictures. I looked at my brother's wedding photo, taken eighteen years ago. The bride and groom are in the middle, surrounded by the whole family ... and my mother had cut me out of the picture. That sure called up a moment—a very long moment.

With all of the stuff that I had gone through—for years—part of me had always wondered, *Did I make this stuff up? Was it real?* Staring at the photos I thought, *Holy crap, this is* exactly *what it was like.*

A few photos down the wall from the cut-out wedding photo was a family picture taken when I was probably six years old. I almost said it out loud—*One of these things does not look like the others.* There's this little blonde-haired, blue-eyed girl on the corner of the picture, and everybody else is bigger, with brown hair and brown eyes. Wow. When I saw that photo, that's exactly how I felt when I was a little kid. All those feelings—'I don't fit. This doesn't look right.'

What did that little girl do that was so wrong that she needed to be treated so horribly?

■ ■ ■

As a baby, I was adopted into a Mormon family. They had three biological children, and then lost their fourth child to SIDS—Sudden Infant Death Syndrome. I don't know that my mom had ever fully recovered from her grief. I guess they tried adopting kids to see if it helped. I was their third adoption, and the youngest of the family. What I do know is that my adoption was different. My sister and my brother and I are all adopted from different families and backgrounds, but mine was different. That was all I was told.

Growing up, my oldest brother was a very angry child. He was ten years older than me. I remember from about the time I was five or six, he started taking his anger out on me. I was the easiest target. I'd do ... *whatever*; it would set him off, and then he would beat me up. I'd be in a corner trying to get away, and my parents never really intervened or did anything about it. I figured it was because my dad was a very angry man—one time he knocked me clear across the room.

I always felt like anything I did was wrong. I felt like I didn't really matter, that my life wasn't of any value. One sister was Aboriginal, so my dad took a big interest in her background and culture. And my adopted brother had meningitis as a baby, so my mom really took to him. What I would find out later is that I'm actually my adopted father's niece's daughter. It was a private, in-family adoption, and my adopted mother didn't want anything to do with me. It kind of got forced on her.

Because my dad was raised Mormon, he was like, 'We've got to do it. We've got to do the right thing.'

It may have been the 'right' thing to do, but my adopted mother absolutely despised my birth mother.

We moved quite a bit until I was ten years old, and then we made a big move to the east coast. My dad took us three younger kids, and we drove across Canada, which was a very cool experience. My dad did a really good job of trying to make it an adventure. We finally arrived at this house that my mom had a contractor build. She had purchased the land years before, and the outside of the house looked great, but there was nothing inside. It wasn't finished at all.

In making that move, we went from living in the city, middle class, to the middle of the boonies, dirt poor. My mom could only find a job working at an office making $5.25 an hour.

I wasn't even a teenager, almost twelve, and there had been a lot of transition, a lot of change. I felt like I couldn't do anything right. School for me was really, really easy, but I got bored easily, so I would always get into trouble, whether it be for talking or creating a disturbance. Most of the time it wasn't my fault.

I had come from across the country and was now living in a small town. I was 'from away,' and I was different. I spoke differently. That was more than enough to set the bullying in motion. The bus ride to school, at school, and the bus ride all the way home, I got tormented.

I was never a cliquey person. There was never any group I really fit into. I was pretty miserable all the time. By the time I was thirteen years old, I had already attempted suicide. I tried taking a full bottle of Tylenol a couple of times. I tried to slit my wrists, and I was already acting out on anorexic behavior. I think a lot of it was just crying out for help, just wanting somebody to notice me, somebody to care enough to intervene. But I felt ignored.

■ ■ ■

When I was thirteen years old, my dad started to touch me inappropriately. It began when I had injured my back at my grandmother's place. We were junking firewood—stacking it, splitting it, sweeping it from the basement floor. And I guess I was sweeping wrong. Somehow, I hurt my back. My dad started giving me massages, and it was then that he would touch me inappropriately. My mom witnessed it at one point. She had come out of the bath, and I was in their room while my dad was giving me a massage. My mom told me later, the look that he gave her, it just looked like pure evil.

There was a bunch of changes, and eventually my dad went back out west. I don't know all the reasons why. Me and my mom started getting close, so I told her what happened— about Dad touching me. And she's like, 'I can totally see that. I believe you.' She was wanting to completely separate from him, and she confronted him on the phone.

All of a sudden, I'm handed the phone, and my sisters are yelling at me, calling me a liar.

My dad's yelling, 'Why would you do this? Why would you say this?'

Then a few months later, I came home from school, and my dad was there. He had moved back home with us.

That was kind of it for me. And I thought, *Okay, this is the reality. Nobody believes me ... and he's just going to continue because he's a master manipulator.* He had been telling my mom that I had inherited my birth mother's mental illness, and that these were a bunch of stories I was making up.

School wasn't any help either. They were saying that I had some behavioral issues and mental health issues, but nobody had ever asked me directly what was going on. They had me see a psychiatrist who just prescribed a lot of drugs. Nobody ever asked me why I was trying to kill myself or why I wasn't eating or what was going on that would cause me to act out with such destructive behavior. Nobody. Nobody did.

■ ■ ■

When my dad moved back in with us, things changed with me and my mom. She would go to work, come home, and she'd go to her room or be in the garden. She lived like a hermit. There was no real interaction with her. It's like I just didn't trust her anymore.

By the time I was fourteen, I was smoking cigarettes, and I'd get my cigarettes from a little store two houses down from where we lived. There was a pool table, and people would hang out. I started going there to get stuff to bring home, and after a while the owner started to take an interest in me. He was really nice, and kind. He told me he'd pay me $5 an hour, and that's pretty good money for a kid! I started working for him when I was almost fifteen. He had me at the cash register. What I later learned was he was actually the local bootlegger. All the guys would come there to drink after work.

It seemed like a good place to be, rather than being at home. I'd go there straight from school and be there 'til 10 or 11 o'clock at night. But I never saw any of the money I earned because I was always getting my cigarettes and stuff, so I had a tab. He always said I owed more than I earned. He then started to pay extra attention to me. I'd be behind the counter, and he'd come and rub himself against me. He was continuously pushing the boundaries. Things progressed; he started coming on to me, eventually asking me to perform oral sex. I hadn't had any experience, but I felt like I almost had to—like I owed him something.

Once I started performing oral sex on him, he then suggested I start doing that for money. He'd say, 'I have a couple of guys that are really interested in you. They find you really attractive, and you can make some money doing this. It's not a big deal. You don't have to have sex with them. You could do this and charge some decent money.'

I tried so hard to tell him, 'No. I don't want to.' But he just kept pursuing it and pushing it, and I kept saying no.

Then came the, 'You owe me. You owe me more. You owe me money—a lot. This is the easiest and fastest way to pay it down.'

I had never received any money from him, either for working, or for the oral sex. I'm thinking, *Okay, fine, if this is the only answer to the problem, then this is what I need to do.*

He went and set things up with a couple of men. I had to walk down the highway a bit, and they came and picked me up. It was a very terrifying experience. I didn't know what I was doing. I went and performed oral sex on them in their truck, and they dropped me off just down the road from the bootlegger's. I went into the store; he took the money from me, and then I went home.

This happened a few times. Then there was another guy who was interested in me, so the store owner set that up and convinced me that having sex with one of these guys would be okay. It was horrific and disturbing, but at the same time I didn't know anything else.

I didn't know that there was a way out. I didn't feel like I could talk to anybody about what was happening. Nobody was there to see how upset I was or that I was out until the middle of the night. Or that I was withdrawing more and more.

With all of this stuff going on with this bootleg bugger, I was on a road to complete destruction. By the time I was seventeen, he was trying to convince me to move to a bigger city in the province. He had a place there, an apartment. There were a couple of women that lived there, and I could go live with them and make more money doing this kind of stuff. Everything in me is like, *This is wrong. This is really,* really *wrong.* But the next thought was, *I need to get outta here. I need to leave. I need to.* I was being tormented and beat up by the girls at school, and I just couldn't take it anymore.

I went to the guidance counsellor, signed some papers, and I waited for the bus. And that was it. I was done with school. I think it was a month before my eighteenth birthday. But that same day my dad had found my pot stash. He had also found my journals, and I caught him reading them when I got home from school.

I said, 'So ... maybe now's a good time to tell me who my birth mother is.' By this point I already knew it was a private adoption, but I didn't know any details.

He tells me, 'Susan[4] is your birth mother.'

I knew her as a kid. She'd be at family functions. She had two other daughters with her first husband, who were two and four years older than me.

My dad asked, 'Would you like me to contact her, and see if she wants contact with you?'

What I didn't know is that he and my adopted mom were supposed to tell me all of this when they were together. When Mom found out that we'd had this talk without her, she was pretty pissed off.

■ ▩ ▩

There were a few other situations that I got myself into, with people who were criminals, people who had been in and out of jail. I was getting the feeling they were afraid I was going to go to the police and report things. There was a threat against the family home. I was basically told that I needed to keep my mouth shut, and I needed to do what I was told, or they were going to burn our house down. I knew I needed to leave. Arrangements were made for me to fly out west in December. I would go to live with my birth mother, go back to school, get a job, and go from there. But I didn't know this woman at all.

My birth mother was in her third or fourth marriage by this point. I would soon find out she was a Wicca, a fully practicing Wicca, and not a healthy person at all. She was very abusive in the few weeks that I was there—both physically and emotionally. And she was super-controlling. She handed me a list of things that I needed to do every day and every week. I was to be out of the house at six in the morning, and I wasn't allowed back until six in the evening, when she got home from work. And she would print me off a hundred résumés, and I was expected to go and hand these résumés out. We're talking northern Alberta—it's December-January, freakin' cold.

What I didn't realize at the time is that my mother's house was 93rd Street and 111th Ave, which is like the hood of the city. It's also where all the women work the streets. So here I am, six in the morning, standing at the bus stop, and a couple of cars come by and stop and try to get me to come over. And I'm like, 'What the hell? I'm nearly three thousand miles from home, and it's the same shit all over again.'

One day, I found the local YMCA. It's a drop-in for youth, and you can go in and just hang out and go on the computer. I met a few people there and started to go hang out with them after hours. One night I didn't come home. That night, I was gang-raped by one of the guys and a couple of his friends. I finally got out of there at seven in the morning, got on a bus, went to my birth mother's house, and jumped in the shower. When I came out, she lost her shit on me. She jumped on top of me and started slapping me for not coming home. Then she kicked me out.

I didn't tell her what had happened. I was too terrified. If I got slapped around for being out all night … what would she do if she knew the whole story?

My adopted sister lived several miles away; I tried calling her, but she wasn't answering the phone. I had to go back to the same place where I was raped because it was the only place I knew I could stay until I could get hold of my sister or some-body to help me. 'Cause, I mean, I was eighteen, it's January, and I'm homeless.

A couple of days later, my sister finally answered. She said, 'You can come stay with me for a week, but then you have to figure something out.' My sister and I went to my mother's house, and she had all my stuff in garbage bags sitting outside on the porch. I moved my stuff to my sister's place, and then my oldest sister called me up and said, 'Why don't you come to Winnipeg and live with me? It'll be good.' I'd started cleaning houses, and with my first paycheck, I bought a bus ticket, and I jumped on the bus and moved to Winnipeg.

■ ■ ■

At this point, I hadn't experienced hard drugs. I was drinking and smoking pot and cigarettes. I was taking some pills every now and then, but I hadn't really had much experience with anything beyond that.

Things seemed like they just kept getting worse. Finding any sort of freedom or comfort was just not possible at this point in my life. I had my first experience with cocaine in Winnipeg, and I continued to find myself in dangerous situations where I was sexually assaulted. But I met a guy, so I figured, *It's going to be okay now.* I wasn't living with my sister anymore; I was working two different jobs and living in a house with a couple of other young people. Basically I'd go to work and come home and party.

This guy seemed really cool, and it didn't take long before he moved in with me. He was definitely an alcoholic, but I didn't quite understand that at the time. He was going through a 2/4 or a 3/6 of beer a day,[5] and at one point he said to me, 'I think you have a problem with pot.' Whatever.

I figured life was going to get better. I'm working, I'm making money, I've got a roof over my head. I believed my boyfriend did the best he could. I believed he loved me. I believed he cared about me. I mean, he wasn't beating me or anything at this point. I had hope, right? Hope that somebody out there loved me and cared about me.

I didn't know it, but I had gotten pregnant, and I was maybe two, three weeks in. All of a sudden, I was bleeding profusely for thirteen days, and yet it didn't dawn on me. I finally went to the doctor, and he told me that I'd miscarried. For me that was devastating because I had always wanted kids. I wanted to do something better. I wanted to be a good parent. I wanted something to love and just do it right. I knew I just got the shitty end of the stick, and I hoped I could provide something better.

I was really upset about the whole thing—especially that I didn't know that I was pregnant. But it was also a blessing, in the fact that I was drinking and getting high and not taking care of myself. I was nineteen. I tried to get pregnant a few times after that, but it never happened.

A little later, I found out that my boyfriend had warrants out for his arrest in Ontario. His family wanted him to come back to Ontario and get them sorted. He decided to move back to Ottawa and to start serving weekends. I stayed in Winnipeg and moved back in with my sister for a bit. The plan was that I would move to Ottawa as soon as he was done serving out his weekends.

He had gotten a job with his brother and things were potentially going really well. Eventually I got on a bus and moved with my two cats. My boyfriend and a buddy of his had gotten an apartment above a Chinese medicine shop. The place was trashed. The previous people must've just walked out. There was garbage everywhere. The place was infested with mice ... but the partying continued.

We were hosting poker nights, with lots of alcohol and cocaine. We'd be playing all weekend, and then I'd go to work at Seven-Eleven, a local convenience store. My boyfriend had proposed to me when we were in Winnipeg, so at this point he was my fiancé. But I ended up getting an STD from him.

I was going to school and had gotten myself upgraded in English and math and had started a law clerk program in Ottawa. I was still smoking pot and doing cocaine every now and then, but I was excelling at school and really enjoying it. My boyfriend then got a job offer in Edmonton. He'd become very emotionally and mentally abusive, and there'd been a couple of physical altercations, but nothing too serious, at least in my mind. But then, something clicked in me—if he goes, it's over.

I wasn't ready. I decided that I would not stay for my second year at school. I moved to Edmonton to be with my fiancé, committed to trying to make us work. He was now dealing cocaine, and immediately my cocaine use goes up to every day. By December of that year I was addicted to crack cocaine. And things with my boyfriend had become more physically abusive. Eventually, we lost everything. We were evicted from our apartment, again.

My boyfriend and I split up for good, and I was left alone and homeless. None of my family wanted me to live with them. They didn't know that I was an addict at this point; even so, with all of the chaos in my life, I don't blame them.

I was living under a bridge, and I could not stop using. For so long I'd been saying, '*He* has the problem. It's not me. If he's not in my life, I wouldn't be doing this.' Now I had my own circle of people who were using, and I was right in there with them.

The next bad decision I made was with an older guy who lived in the building I had lived in. I started selling myself to him to pay for my drugs.

One of the things I learned early on with the bootleg bugger was a way to escape my physical self during those times. I disengaged and just prayed that I wouldn't be taking my last breath, that this wouldn't be how my life was going to end. That was one of my 'life prayers'—that I wouldn't end up being a Jane Doe, especially towards the end of my addiction—because I didn't know anybody, and nobody would care if I went missing. I very well could have been a Jane Doe.

Even so, I just continued to use. I got another job, working at Tim Hortons, a local coffee shop. As soon as I got my first paycheck I went out, and I got high and didn't show up for work on the weekend. I spent all my money on crack. While I was coming down off the high, I had two thoughts come into my head. The first one was to kill myself because I didn't know how to stop. It seemed like every time something good would happen, I would find a way to self-destruct, or find myself in situations that would create more harm. The next thought I had was to go get help.

■ ■ ■

I had no experience with any of the Twelve Step programs or treatment centers. What I did know was that my grandfather was an alcoholic and died an alcoholic. I figured that if I didn't do something, that was how my life would end. The next day I found myself at the Alberta Alcohol and Drug office, filling out their paperwork. I then sat there for three hours until I finally saw a counsellor. She heard my story and asked, 'Well, what do you want to do?'

I said, 'I don't know—lock me up. It's the only way I'm going to stop.'

They put me on a waiting list to get into treatment. I couldn't stay sober during that time. When they finally had space for me, I went into treatment. That was December 18th of 2006. I haven't used drugs or alcohol since.

But I was terrified when I showed up at the treatment center. I didn't know what to expect. I've never felt so alone. My sister drove me to the rehab, but she wouldn't even come to the door. She just dropped me off in the parking lot.

I walked in and had no idea what was in store. I didn't know what 'recovery' meant. I had gotten myself into some pretty scary situations—when you show up at a place you don't know, you don't know what potentially could happen. The rehab felt like that all over again. But I was desperate with desperation, just wanting life to get better. Rehab changed everything in me. When I walked into the treatment center I had nothing, but when I walked out, I had a bunch of tools to help me to move forward.

I was there for four weeks, and I left there and went right into a women's recovery house. I was there for three and a half months. During that time, I made a whole series of bad decisions. I had gotten into a very physically violent relationship. The guy was in active addiction still, and I was always trying to save him. I was always there, cleaning up the mess.

He was very, very violent. One night while I was still in the treatment house, he got into an argument with his mom and was so mad he proceeded to punch four holes in his windshield, with me in the car. But that wasn't enough for me to see that this is not a good situation. Of course not. No—not for little Miss Helpful. *We're going to keep going, and I'm going to save him.* By the grace of God, I stayed sober through it all. That was all I had at that point—my sobriety.

I knew my boyfriend was relapsing, again. I got up enough courage to tell him, 'I have zero tolerance. If you're going to use, you don't come back.' We got into a huge fight. I threatened to call the cops to have him removed, and he jumped up and had me pinned against the wall. His hands were around my throat, and I'm thinking, *This guy's going to kill me.* Somehow, I managed to get out of that position and broke free of him, and I left.

The guy proceeded to stalk me. I went and got a restraining order, and he got arrested on it a couple of times. The last time I had to go to court, he was stirring up such a stink that the judge looked at me and said, 'If this is some kind of game that you're playing and something happens to you, it's not our fault.'

My ex-boyfriend had told the court that I was stalking him! That was devastating. I was in the courtroom by myself and the judge is telling me this—and I'm terrified of this guy—I'm shaking and trembling and crying. It nearly did my head in. I'm the one at risk, and my ex-boyfriend is getting the sympathy!

■ ■ ■

All I knew was to continue to do the work I needed to do. I started going to the sexual assault center for counselling. I started to do some family of origin counselling. Over the years, every member of my family had cut me off, even though they didn't know I was an addict. When I went into recovery, they cut off all contact with me. As part of my recovery I tried to make amends. I wrote each member of my family a letter, but when I went to drop them off, they just didn't want anything to do with me.

When I look back, I always thought I was the black sheep of the family. I thought there was something wrong with me—I was the problem. Now I'm changing my life for the better. It seemed like my family couldn't handle that. But I thrived in recovery.

I had started going to the Salvation Army Crossroads Church in 2008, and on Father's Day of 2009, I accepted Jesus into my life. The officer was preaching about forgiving our fathers—and that God is our ultimate Father. I was weeping through the whole service. I finally went up to what we call the 'mercy seat.' I cried out, 'God, I need you. I need to forgive my biological father. I need to forgive my adopted father, and I need to accept you, God, as my ultimate Father.'

We have prayer teams at the front of the church. I went and asked if they'd pray for me, and I accepted Christ into my life. From that point forward, things started to change. I got more interested in the Bible, and I became really involved as part of the church. Not long after, I felt a calling on my life to go into ministry. I was preparing to go to training college in Winnipeg. But first I had to do some discipleship training in downtown Vancouver.

Six months in, I was hospitalized. Basically, I had a nervous breakdown, and the doctors told me I have bipolar disorder. That was six years ago, and I've been on treatment since. That's taken priority in my life because for me, my mental health is related to everything, and I've watched so many people with mental health issues go off their meds or try to self-treat, and it's just not worth it. Unfortunately, I ended up with side effects as a result of the medication. I have what they called 'drug-induced Parkinson's.'

I felt so alone. I felt like so many people had let me down all my life. I even felt that way with people within the church. When I got diagnosed with bipolar, it seemed like a lot of people just stopped being a part of my life. That was really, really difficult.

On January 1st of 2017, I set myself a goal—to read the Bible all the way through before Christmas. By the end of the year my relationship with God was so much closer and better, and I realized that no matter how other people treated me, I needed to be consistent in my own journey, and see how much God could change my life. It was the most amazing experience that year, of just drawing close to God, of spending that time every morning. It's gotten me through so much.

I was asked a long time ago if I would change anything in my life from my past, and the easiest answer to that is *no*. Not because I don't wish for a world where there's no violence or assault. I say *no* because it's all mapped me into the person I am today. It's all contributed to the way I work with people, the way I communicate. I believe that we're not going to get more than we can handle. For me, I guess I just managed to be able to handle a lot more than anybody ever should.

■ ■ ■

There is one more thing I didn't talk about, but I feel like maybe I should…

Between fifteen and seventeen, I had a teacher who started a romantic relationship with me. For the longest time, I never thought that was a bad thing. I had confided in this teacher—we spent a lot of time talking—and then one day he made the move. I just followed suit 'cause at this point I already had so much experience. I knew what men want, and I'd learned that it's far easier to comply than it is to fight.

For years, I never wanted to look at the relationship with that teacher as a bad thing because I wanted to keep something good. But as time goes on, I've learned that the reality is, his behavior was completely inappropriate on so many levels. I was in such a vulnerable, broken place that there was no way that I could make any decision. If I could talk to my sixteen-year-old self now, I would tell myself, 'No matter what, it's wrong! No matter what, he's taking advantage of you when you're in a vulnerable place, and it's wrong.'

Speaking out and telling somebody about it would have been the right decision. I didn't have to live all those years in fear and shame. It wasn't my shame to carry.

YOU KNOW HOW
MEN ARE

I've been in this industry long enough to see when the boat gets rocked, you lose your job so quick. Everyone in the club is afraid of the power of the men who work there. ... Women get scared because they don't want to lose their jobs. And who do you turn to?[1]

LILY, NIGHTCLUB STRIPPER

A 2018 posting in the *Trafficking Justice Blog* discussed the pros and cons of strip clubs. One woman argued it was "completely acceptable for her husband to go and that females just needed to learn this was what men do." Further rationalizations were offered:

"It's no big deal."

"It's a rite of passage for 18-year-old boys. I'd rather that than hiring a 'hooker.'"

"Look, the dancer I spoke to last night wants to dance. She's paying for her college tuition."[2]

But, there are those who know otherwise. In January, 2000, David Sherman, a former manager of various strip clubs, testified before the Michigan House Committee on Ethics and Constitutional Law. He said that it isn't long before the dancers

> realize how much easier this job is being drunk, high, or both. [They're] working until 2 a.m. in the morning ... deep into the club scene and on the road to hard times and self-destruction. At this point, school, family, and friends as well as everything else they once had fades into a world that no longer exists for them. ... They become society's throwaway people. People used up— degraded, abused, and even sold by the people who own these establishments. Sadly, these young ladies over time, little by little, become manipulated, controlled and finally destroyed by a world that our communities have closed their eyes to.[3]

And when stripping is "no big deal," the normalization of strip clubs—both for customer and provider—ignores the fact that stripping increases the likelihood of sexual assault. As one who formerly worked in a strip club, Kjersti Bohmer "estimates that nearly *85% of women working in the strip club are survivors of sexual violence* and may experience another form of it on every shift they work."[4] Timea Nagy, also a survivor, says that "as long as [sexual exploitation] is a dirty little secret, it will continue to flourish in the dark, like a cockroach."[5]

Comparing sexual exploitation to a cockroach is particularly suggestive. Just like sexual exploitation, cockroaches are a worldwide phenomenon.[6] Both sexual exploitation and cockroaches thrive in a wide range of environments—any area where food, water, and shelter are available. Both sexual exploitation and cockroaches spread contamination and disease wherever they go.

The difference is, cockroaches run away when they're exposed to light.

■ ■ ■

There are certain neighborhoods that are considered so rough, Domino's Pizza refuse to deliver orders. Some are so rough, the police won't answer call-outs after dark. A girl named Harmony grew up in one of those neighborhoods, in a chaotic home in Venice, California. Her mother was a cocaine addict, and had a boyfriend she met at a Narcotics Anonymous meeting.

One night when Harmony was eight, someone broke into their home and brutally beat her mother. He was wearing brass knuckles. Though her mother managed to call 911 before she lost consciousness, it took the police three days to respond to the call. Harmony remembers answering the door when the police arrived. They said they were there to investigate "the disturbance." It wasn't the only "disturbance" Harmony remembers.

■ ■ ■

I WAS SEXUALLY ABUSED THROUGHOUT my life by both men and women, starting from when I was five. Over time, I took on a shame-based identity. I felt like there was something really wrong with me. It created a great sense of insecurity, and it created a distorted sense of value. Especially on into my teen years, I felt that my only value was my sexuality. That was the only thing that I really received any attention or recognition for.

One of my abusers was my mother's boyfriend. My mom knew what was going on—he made sexual advances towards me in front of my mother, and she didn't stop him. I told her that he kept coming into my bedroom at night, and I asked her to stop him. She wouldn't. It wasn't that she was horrible or bad; she just taught me what *she* learned when she was a young girl being abused—that it was my fault.

'If you didn't wear tank tops, and you didn't wear shorts, this wouldn't be happening. You know how men are.' That's literally what she would say to me. I started to believe that there was something inherently wrong with me that kept attracting that kind of attention.

I didn't like my life very much. I remember beginning to contemplate suicide and writing suicide notes at around eight years old. I put the first one in my jewelry box, and for me it was kind of like—if it ever gets bad enough, I'll follow through on it. But no one knew about it.

When I was around ten or eleven I started playing with razor blades and imagining what it would be like to bleed to death. One day, I was alone in the house, and I collected all the knives from the kitchen. I was deciding which one I was going to use to cut my wrists when the dog started barking. My mom had come home. She had a backup beeper on her truck. That's what set the dog off. In a panic, I threw all the knives in my brother's backpack.

I didn't think about taking them out of his backpack, because I was so scared of getting caught. The next day, *he* got caught at school with all these knives, and the school called my mom. She pulled us out of school, we're in the car, and Mom asks him, 'Noah, did you put those knives in your backpack?'

And he's saying, 'No! I didn't do it. I didn't do it!'

And I'm just being quiet.

Mom pulled up to Thrifty's where we'd get ice cream, and she says, 'I'm not gonna buy you ice cream until you tell me the truth.'

So he says, 'Fine.' He's five years old, and he says, 'I put the knives in the backpack.'

I'm sitting there looking at him like, *What? I did that*!

He starts crying, and Mom says, 'What's wrong? What's happening with you that you're playing with knives?'

He starts saying that he was thinking of ending his life, and I'm thinking, *Are you kidding me*? I couldn't believe it—he got all this sympathy and everything, and I'm just sitting there like—*Wow*!

I was fourteen when I actually attempted suicide. I started taking a bottle of pills. What's really crazy is that I had a friend who lived all the way out in Hollywood, and I lived in Venice— twelve miles away—and he just showed up at my bedroom door. He interrupted my suicide attempt! I'd only taken fifteen or so pills, and I felt pretty loopy, but I didn't go to hospital.

Another time, I tried to cut my wrists. I was really, really high on marijuana and alcohol, and I was in the bathroom and grabbed a safety razor. I was scraping it back and forth across my wrist, and it was cutting me, but I couldn't understand why it wasn't slicing through my skin like I thought it would. I was really angry because it wasn't working the way I wanted it to. This was at a friend's house, and they realized I'd been in the bathroom a long time. I don't think I thought that one through because I was so high—like the fact that I could be found so easily. It was the first time that it happened that way. The other times I was alone, and no one else knew.

■ ■ ■

I ran away from home when I was thirteen. It was the only way I knew to get away from the abuse. My mom realized that I wasn't going to come back until her boyfriend was gone, so she finally kicked him out. I came home, only to find that she had gone with him. They moved to Canada for three months, and left me and my eight-year-old brother with $20 and a book of food stamps. We went through that pretty fast, so I started stealing food from the liquor store.

That summer, I lost my virginity to the first boy who told

me he loved me. A couple of months later he broke up with me, but he thought he still deserved boyfriend privileges. He raped me more than thirty times over the course of the next year. I blamed myself for his behavior because, in a twisted way, I thought that if it was my fault, then I wasn't a victim.

Later that same year, I became involved with an older boy in my neighborhood. When he was around, I didn't have to worry about my first 'boyfriend,' and I didn't have to steal. The older guy would buy my brother and me food and look after us.

'Anybody messes with you, I got your back,' he would tell me.

I looked at him and saw my knight in shining armor. I became really, really attached to him. I had no idea that it was his intention to exploit me, and I never intended to have a relationship with him. I didn't see him that way at all. I didn't think he saw me that way either. Then one night I wagered my body in a game of cards. I lost. We had sex.

As he and I became closer relationally, he also became more abusive and controlling. But I was so desperate for the attention and presence of a 'loving' man in my life, I mistook his control for care and concern. I heard his abuse and hurtful words as validation for my self-loathing, and weirdly, the more abusive he became, the more I became attached to him.

He told me that nobody else would ever put up with me, and I believed him. I came to believe that I needed him. That I would die without him. I was 'his.' He had convinced me of this.

Why did I stay with him? He never raped me. That was more than I could say about any other male in my life.

■ ■ ■

At fifteen, I was giving him whatever money I earned at my job at the beach selling Greenpeace t-shirts. By the time I was seventeen, I was fully supporting him by stealing from the cash register at work. When I was eighteen, his mother had a stroke, and we moved in with her to take care of her. Financial pressure built as her medical bills piled up, and my boyfriend's spending habits continued to escalate. By the time I was nineteen years old, I was over $35,000 in debt. I had lost all financial control, and though I looked for a second job, none of them could make ends meet. My boyfriend was putting more pressure on me to steal in order to pay our bills. His rationale was that I would be less likely to get caught than he would. I was reluctant to do this because I was legally an adult, and I was afraid of ending up with a permanent record.

I was young, naïve, hopeless, and saw no other options. I did not have the dream of growing up to be a stripper. But it seemed like a better alternative to theft, fraud, and the risk of going to jail. When my boyfriend and I started talking about it, I didn't want to do it—I *absolutely* did not want to do it. My boyfriend told me that I would only have to work at a club for a couple of months in order to pay off some of the bills. Then I could return to a 'normal' life.

Besides work, I had applied for financial aid at a junior college, and did really well at school. I was earning scholarships, but I still had this huge debt. I had a psychology professor that I trusted and respected, and I told him, 'I'm having real financial troubles, and everybody is telling me I should strip, but I don't want it to ruin any chances I have of becoming a psychologist. I don't want it to get in the way of my career path. What do you think?'

He said, 'Well, it's not like you have to put it on your résumé ... I don't really see a problem with it.'

He took away all the excuses I had for not doing it.

As I was getting ready to walk out, he asked, 'What club are you thinking about working at?'

I don't know why I told him, and ... sure enough, a few months after I started stripping, he was one of the guys in the audience.

I needed to talk to some other people, so I went to my boss, and I told her I was thinking about stripping.

I was earning slightly above minimum wage, and she said, 'Why not? If I looked like you, I'd do it. It's not that big a deal.' The underlying message I heard was, 'Use your body—use what God gave you. Go on, make some money!' That's one of the things pimps will tell girls when they're trying to convince girls to sell themselves.

I didn't see my boyfriend as a pimp, but once I started working at the club, I'd come home and give him all my money, even though *I* earned it. He had brought me to the place where I had convinced myself that I didn't deserve it anyway. I figured that the more dependent on me he was, the less likely he would be to leave me.

■ ■ ■

The first night at the strip club, they told me to go see the DJ, and he asked me what my name was. He turned around to write my name on a whiteboard on the wall, and I said, 'Harmony.' But seeing it there in black and white, it just freaked me out. I said, 'No, no, no. Take it down, take it down! I'm Monique.' From that point on, I became Monique.

Monique was whoever the customers wanted Monique to be. Harmony wouldn't do the things Monique would do.

I led a double life. I was a quiet, conservative college student by day, and someone else's fantasy by night. Gradually, I began to lose sight of who I was, and became lost in the makeup, stilettos, and the glare of the stage lights. I felt fragmented and compartmentalized. Everything I said to the customers was a lie. I didn't tell the truth about where I went to school; I didn't tell the truth about my dog's real name! I even had a fake 'real' name.

So I had my real name, and my fake name, and a fake 'real' name, and a fake school I went to, and a fake neighborhood I lived in, and a fake life. It was the only way I could feel safe.

The fear of rejection and other people's judgment kept me isolated from the outside world. The only people I had any contact with were other women at the strip club, the club customers, and my abusive boyfriend—and that isolation made it easier for him to control me. He dictated my every move, but it seemed like anything could set him off: not enough ice in his Mountain Dew; too much ice in his Mountain Dew; cold French fries; if the house wasn't clean enough; if I made too much noise while I cleaned it. It felt like I could never get it right.

He started sleeping with my co-workers at the club, and he got them to give him their money as well. Just when I thought things couldn't get any worse, he got another girl pregnant. I only found out because I came across another woman's clothing in our bedroom closet. He talked me into letting her move into our home. Crazy? It was, but all sense of 'self' was gone. I had no boundaries left. And to make matters worse, he was now using me to help exploit other women. But I was afraid to leave him. I didn't see a way out. I felt completely trapped. I felt like I couldn't do anything to change the situation or what was happening to me.

The emptiness I felt inside seemed infinite, and my self-image continued to decline. Over the course of the next three years, being a stripper became my identity, and the work at the club confirmed my perceptions of men—that they all were inherently perverted and sick. I learned to use stripping as a way to take back control of my sexuality. I got to the place where I felt like I had the upper hand. I learned to exploit for myself. I used the very thing that men had already exploited … my body.

But stripping is hard. If you don't act all gaga over a customer, they feel like they have the right to give you a piece of their mind—they'd call me all sorts of crude and filthy names—and when they'd do that, I'd kick their drink into their lap.

My view of the world was tarnished. I couldn't go anywhere without thinking that people saw me in a sexual way. I felt reduced to an object. In my daily life, I'd wear sweatpants and baggy tops, sunglasses … I didn't want to be seen. I didn't want to be recognized. I didn't want to be looked at. If a man stared, something would rise up—'You're looking at me, and you're not even *paying* me?'

If a guy touched me or grabbed me while I was dancing and said something like, 'What would you do if I … (fill in the blank)?', I'd say, 'I'll take my stiletto off and beat you over the head.'

Often, the guy would go ahead and do it anyway. I gave him fair warning that I have a boundary here, and he just crossed that boundary, and there were a couple of times the police were called by a customer that I'd beat up, and I'd tell the cops, 'He assaulted me!' The cops would look at me like I was crazy.

■ ■ ■

There was a woman who worked with me at the club, and she moved in such beautiful ways. She was a former ballerina, and I wanted to dance like she did, so I signed up for a ballet class. That's where I met my friend Hayley[7] ... her friendship changed my life. She had respect for herself, and she had boundaries; she had purpose and she was free—just so *free*! She treated me as a person, and she genuinely loved me. I never felt like a project. She wasn't trying to fix me or change me, and she never looked down on me. I never felt that she judged me for the crazy life I was living. She would take me for a frozen yogurt and talk about normal life stuff. She became my first true friend. It's the first time I ever experienced unconditional love. I didn't know what that was—but I liked it!

I found out that she was a Christian, and I thought, *Oh my gosh, I've ruined this friendship.* I didn't know a lot about Christians, but I was pretty sure they didn't like strippers. But she had something I was missing, and I figured it was probably this whole 'God thing.' She never tried to convert me—I would have been really turned off by that. But she did invite me to go to church with her.

When I first started going, people would ask me, 'What's your name?' It was a totally innocent question, but I'd swallow hard and answer, 'Harmony.' I'd almost feel startled to hear my real name because outside of church my only contact was with my pimp boyfriend, the customers at the club, and the other girls dancing there, and nobody called me Harmony. *Everybody* called me Monique. All I knew was that I wanted to be in church every time the doors were open because I now had a relationship with God, and my heart started changing, my mind started changing ... I started to believe that I was loveable, and that I had value.

But I had this other life. I would go to church on a Wednesday night, and then to the strip club afterwards for my shift—because that was my job.

I remember one night being at the club, and I got all emotional. I started crying and that was really unusual for me. I was so disconnected from every emotion except for anger. I didn't cry! At church the pastor had been preaching about God's plans and purposes for us, that God has a destiny for each and every one of us, and I was thinking, *If I was created with a purpose, this can't be it. This, here, was not what I was put on this planet to do.* I got on stage for my first set, and I looked around, and all of a sudden I felt naked. For the first time. I'd been up there naked for years, but all of a sudden, I *felt* naked. I felt exposed and vulnerable. All these men were looking at me, but they didn't *see* me. I'm here, naked, and they don't *see* me.

After the set I went back to the dressing room and told myself, *Get a grip. Shake it off. You have to make money. You can't quit. Get out there and hustle.* I'd go back out on the floor, and I'd think, *I can't quit. God, I don't want to be here, but I can't quit.* I never saw anybody quit. *One* girl—in the whole time I was at the club—and she only quit because she married a rich customer. Other than that, you don't get out. You don't leave.

In the midst of all of that, I felt God say, 'I haven't let you down, and I'm not going to let you down. I'm going to take care of you.'

And with that I just knew it was time to go. I walked up to my manager and said just that: 'I'm going to go.'

He said, 'What do you mean—for the night?'

I said, 'No, I'm quitting.'

I threw all of my clothes out of my locker and said, 'They're all for sale. Everything.' I didn't want anything that would make for an easy way to go back. I walked out of that club, and never went back.

When I drove off that night, I felt *so* free.

In retrospect, I felt free from exploitation. I couldn't have used the word then, but I did realize that my boyfriend *was* my pimp. I did know what he was doing, and what he was doing with *me*. It was the beginning of a new life.

But it was only the beginning of a long healing process. I had to *fight* for my freedom, and I had to do everything I could to make sure I was taking steps towards freedom. One of those was the decision to become abstinent. No more sex.

It's strange now that I look back at it. But that's what I felt—God put abstinence on my heart as my first step towards my new life.

Long story short, I went with my friends to a concert in San Diego, and this guy shared his testimony about being a drug addict and living on the streets, and he said that God had changed his life. I'd never heard a testimony before, so I'd never heard anyone speak so candidly about their past like that. He shared from the Scriptures where Jesus says, 'I'm the vine and you are the branches. If you remain in me you will bear fruit, but apart from me you can do nothing.'[8]

On the way home from the concert, I said to God, 'I am that withered branch. I've tried to live life on my own, and it's not working. What does it mean to abide in you? How can I abide in you? What do I do?'

What I felt God put in my heart was abstinence. I thought it was kind of crazy, but I spent a couple of days looking up every Bible verse on abstinence. I knew that a commitment to abstinence was going to jeopardize my relationship with my boyfriend because I just knew that he wasn't really gonna have it, but I gained so much confidence that this was the next best step for me that I told him, 'I want you to know that I've decided to be abstinent. I'm waiting for marriage.'

He said, 'Then we can't be together.'

I never thought I would be able to get to that place where I'd be willing to release that relationship. But then, doesn't he come back to me and say, 'I want to marry you. I want to be with you.' And all the blah, blah, blah—everything I always thought I wanted to hear from him.

Later that day, I realized that's not what I wanted anymore, that his version of love wasn't what I wanted anymore, and it wasn't enough for me, and it wasn't the real thing.

The first decision I made was abstinence, and knowing what I know now, once I'd broken the soul tie I had with him, it was like it sprung the trap that kept me enslaved. Once I got free there, I was able to take the next step in leaving him.

The morning of my baptism I decided to call him and tell him that our relationship was over. I asked him, 'Please don't contact me, 'cause I want a fresh start.'

He said, 'I don't understand.'

And I said, 'You don't have to understand. You just have to accept it.'

The trouble was, we had a car that was in both of our names, but he wasn't making the payments, and I was getting late notices. That was really bothering me because I was watching my credit rating get ruined. The police wouldn't do anything about it because his name was on the ownership, so it wasn't stolen.

I took the youth pastor from my church to try to get the car back, and my now-ex-boyfriend happened to walk out. He said, 'What are you doing here?'

I told him I wanted my car back.

He grabbed me and threw me against the car and said, 'I'm gonna get my gun, and I'm gonna kill you!'

He went upstairs to get his gun, and my youth pastor said, 'We need to go.'

We left; we called the police, but of course I wasn't going to press charges…

When the cops were about to leave, the female officer who came to take the report said, 'Here, I want you to take this.' It was a domestic violence brochure.

I said, 'I don't need it,' but she said, 'I want you to have it,' and set it down on my coffee table. When she walked out, I picked it up and read it, and for the first time in seven years I realized that I was in an abusive relationship. I was in such a deep state of denial that I didn't even see it.

A little while later, a friend of mine started telling me about her sexual abuse, and that she was reading this book *Beauty for Ashes*, by Joyce Meyer. She was going on and on about how much it was helping her. I hadn't addressed my history of abuse, so I literally just started dissociating right in front of her. I had totally checked out of the conversation because I couldn't be present for it. It was too much for me. Later on, my friend said, 'It was so weird. You're such a compassionate person. Here I was, bearing my soul, and you weren't even listening to me. You looked like you were in another *world*.' I was. I couldn't hear it. I wasn't ready to face my own trauma.

Somehow, I started reading the same book my friend had read, *Beauty for Ashes*, and began addressing my history of sexual abuse. But honestly, that time reading Joyce's book was such a blur. I just remember it was the first time I ever heard someone speak openly about sexual abuse and overcoming it. Joyce Meyer had become somebody I really looked up to, and to see that not only had she experienced sexual abuse, but to learn that it didn't hold her back, and she was now living in freedom—that really inspired me.

And practically, one of the most significant steps her book invited me to take was to forgive my abusers. That was something I never thought I could do. I thought that rape was an unforgivable thing—rape and murder. But through reading that book I decided to take that step and forgive my abusers, and I experienced so much freedom for myself once I did that. That book, *Beauty for Ashes*, it changed my life.

■ ■ ■

In 2003, after several years of working on my recovery, I was sitting in a gas station parking lot about a mile from the airport, waiting for someone's flight to arrive. It happened to be right across the street from the strip club where I used to work. I felt like I was sitting outside a prison that had once held me captive. I knew that there were women working there who felt as trapped and alone as I did. I wanted to do something to support them. I didn't know where to start, so I just started writing handwritten notes on postcards and, night after night, I'd put them on their cars. 'Hey, I've been through what you're going through, and I want you to know that I'm here for you.' I wanted to do that for them because I'm confident that I would not be alive today if someone hadn't reached out to me.

Not long after, I founded Treasures, an outreach and support group for women in the commercial sex industry and victims of sex trafficking. It's the only organization of its kind based in the adult industry capital of the world—the San Fernando Valley of Los Angeles County—and it's one of the first in the nation. It's also one of the few survivor-led organizations in the country. We reach women with the simple message that changed my life: that they are loved, and valued, and purposed, and that support is there for them, if and when they want it, if and when they're ready. We're willing to just show up and love them unconditionally and walk with them through the process of recovery.

Our mission is to reach, restore, and equip exploited women to help them live healthy and flourishing lives. We provide care and outreach to women working in strip clubs, porn, and prostitution, as well as girls in detention centers, and victims of exploitation and trafficking. We have also had the privilege of training outreaches in 120 cities on six continents!

We offer mentoring and therapeutic support groups. We don't try to fix the girls; we don't try to change them. We just love them where they're at, and walk with them along their journey. And I believe that just as there's hope for any woman who's been in the industry, there's hope for the men who've participated in the demand.

For a lot of years, I had a lot of anger towards men, for sure. I didn't see them—any of them—as part of the solution. Just part of the problem. I didn't think that any man could see me or any other woman beyond being sexual objects. I was very confident that it's just the lens through which men see the world, the way they see women. That was what my experience showed me, so it took a long time for me to gain trust that it wasn't true, that there are men who see differently and think differently and are honoring towards women.

In fact, my now-husband, when he first met me, he came up to me after I spoke at our church and said, 'I really have a heart for what you do. I'd love to get involved.'

And I said, 'Nope.' And that was it. That was the end of the conversation.

Later, he told me he felt so dumb—'What was I thinking?!'

About a year later, I had an assistant who encouraged me to allow a friend that she really trusted to intern for us. We really needed help, so I said, 'Sure. He can take out the trash, but he can't be here when women are around, and these are the parameters and here are the boundaries.' He came in, and I slowly started developing trust that there could be men that were good-natured. He encouraged me to let other men join him, and I said, 'As long as you oversee them, and you vet them, and you're the one who's in trouble if anything goes wrong...'

Well, my now-husband was one of the first men to sign up, and it really restored something, not just in me, but in our organization and in the women that we mentor, the women we care for—all of us. Our hearts were being softened, being restored. Seeing these men show so much love and show so much honor and so much value. We'd never seen it before. It brought a lot of healing to all of us.

■ ■ ■

I've come a long way. Fifteen years ago, I would see men walking into the strip club with briefcases of money. I would see men spending their entire Friday paychecks on women working in strip clubs. So much wealth thrown around... But one of my prayers, from the beginning, was that men—and women—who participated in the demand for the commercial sex industry, would redirect their funds towards the recovery and restoration of women who've been affected by the exploitation. We now have a restitution fund—men who were addicted to porn, or going to strip clubs, or hiring women who were in prostitution—they're now our financial partners at Treasures because they want to invest in seeing women restored. It's really awesome.

What I've *done* is not who I *am*. Just because I did that before, doesn't mean I have to do it again. It doesn't mean I have to be the person who did that before.

Stripping changed my life. I was already a super-broken girl going into it, and whatever sense of identity I had left, I felt like stripping stripped it away from me. I didn't think I'd live to see twenty-one. If someone didn't take me out, I was going to take my own life because I felt that hopeless. As hard as those years were, all that I endured, everything I went through—I'm thankful that my pain is now used for a purpose. I wouldn't be doing what I'm doing now if it weren't for all I suffered.

I wrote my story in my memoir, *Scars and Stilettos*. I wanted to uncover some of the realities of the sex industry. Research says that 89 percent of women in the sex industry *want* to leave but don't see any other options. If the sex industry was so empowering for women, we wouldn't see that. We'd see empowered women, not victims who have nowhere else to go.

We can't change what happened yesterday, but we can decide where we go from here.

Harmony's memoir *Scars and Stilettos: The Transformation of an Exotic Dancer* is available from her website:

iamatreasure.com/shop

THEY DON'T CARE ABOUT YOU

Every day of the year, thousands of America's children are coerced into performing sex for hire. Some of these children are brutally beaten and raped into submission. Others are literally stolen off the streets, then isolated, drugged, and starved until they become "willing" participants. Some children are alternately wooed and punished, eventually forming trauma bonds with their exploiters, similar to cases of domestic or intimate partner violence. Still others are living on the streets with no way to survive, except by exchanging sex for food, clothing and shelter.[1]

CALIFORNIA CHILD WELFARE COUNCIL

Being in foster care was the perfect training for commercial sexual exploitation. I was used to being moved without warning, without any say, not knowing where I was going or whether I was allowed to pack my clothes. After years in foster care, I didn't think anyone would want to take care of me unless they were paid. So, when my pimp expected me to make money to support "the family," it made sense to me.[2]

CALIFORNIA CHILD WELFARE COUNCIL

On October 14th, 1982, President Reagan re-branded Nixon's "war on drugs." While largely ignoring powder cocaine (the drug of choice for the upwardly mobile, white population) the focus of Reagan's war targeted America's inner-city crack cocaine problem. His "Tough on Crime" legislation meant that prison populations exploded, as African-Americans were given mandatory life sentences for simple possession and low-level drug dealing. The National Institute on Drug Abuse quantified the disparity:

> Blacks make up twelve percent of the United States' population and constitute thirteen percent of all monthly drug users ... but represent thirty-five percent of those arrested for drug possession ... and seventy-four percent of those sentenced to prison for drug possession.[3]

Prison numbers rose from fifty thousand incarcerations for non-violent drug use in 1980, to four million by 1997. Over 80 percent of crack sentences were imposed on African-Americans.[4]

One of the consequences of the "war on drugs" was a dramatic rise in the number of children put into the foster care system—an increase of 53 percent in five years, from 280,000 in 1986 to 429,000 in 1991. Neglect and caretaker absence prompted an estimated 68 percent of removals. Of the young foster children, 78 percent had at least one parent who was abusing drugs or alcohol.[5]

■ ▧ ▨

Tangelia is the youngest of four children, all born to crack-addicted parents. She was born at the Martin Luther King Jr. Hospital in Willowbank, California, in southern Los Angeles County. Willowbank is predominantly an African-American neighborhood. Tangelia was born prematurely and weighed three pounds, eleven ounces. She was in an incubator for four months and then was released into the care of a social worker. Because of the "war on drugs," her mother wasn't allowed to take her home.

By the time Tangelia was eighteen years old, she had been in as many different foster homes—eighteen—as well as five group homes. While in the care of the Department of Children and Family Services, she was frequently taken to hospital—to attend to six broken bones, two fractures, and one major surgery, all caused by physical abuse. The verbal and emotional abuse, however, went untreated. She was molested and raped by multiple staff and was given several psychotropic medications for depression, insomnia, attention deficit, and bipolar disorders. She was ten years old when her foster father started sexually abusing her.

■ ■ ■

IT WAS CRAZY. PRIOR to me being placed with that family, it had been going on with other girls this family was fostering, but everybody was just, 'Hush.' Everybody was, 'Hush, hush. Just shut up.' On all other counts, it was a normal foster family. The setting felt normal. It was a foster mom, a foster father, and two other foster kids. We went to church on Sundays. We went on outings on Saturdays. I went to school, and the foster mom helped me with my homework during the week. It felt like a normal home, like everything you crave out of a family. Compared to a group home, it was definitely a lot better. The abuse went on for about a year and a half, and I just stayed there. I remember one of the girls saying, 'He does that to everybody.' It's crazy because that was one of the longest placements I had ever stayed in. The only reason we were removed was because one of the girls got caught trying to have sex with someone at school.

They asked her, 'Why do you think this is okay?'

She said, 'It's what I learned at home.' It was our normal.

It's weird. It was the closest to normal I had ever experienced family-wise. After that, I was in two placements a year, sometimes three, just bouncing around from foster home to group home. I was angry. I got into fights. It seemed like every six months, every four months, I had a seven-day notice, and my social worker would be picking me up, taking me to the next placement.

When I was fifteen, I got involved with one of my teachers. We had a thing going on, and again, it felt normal because I'm like, *this is what people do.* I was good at holding secrets. I was sleeping with my teacher and getting good grades for a class I never attended.

Two years later, me and my friends went to a Pride event. My foster mom told me I couldn't go. She was very religious and told me I couldn't go hang out with 'those gay people.'

And I was like, 'I'm going.'

While I was there, I met the man who became my trafficker. One of my friends said, 'Don't pay him any attention—he's too old.'

Definitely, he's older, but I'm like, *this is normal*. For the past two years, I had slept with my teacher, so this is not anything strange. He said he was thirty years old; that was nothing for me. He lied. I found out later he was forty-five.

It started off totally innocent. We exchanged phone numbers. He was from New York and was in LA visiting his family. He returned to New York, and we stayed in contact via Chirp.[6] He bought me a pre-paid phone card and told me that I could call him whenever I wanted. Before he left, he said that he'd come back and see me. He told me he was in Vegas a lot, and that he did a lot of traveling. I never asked, 'What do you do for a living?'

The following January I turned eighteen. That meant I was emancipated and no longer under the care of the State. It also meant that I was homeless, bouncing from couch to couch, crashing wherever I could. All the while, this guy and I were on the phone ... a lot. That's how the grooming started. We had really deep conversations, especially about my family dynamics, and all my foster care placements. I look back now, and I see it was his way of setting the tone for isolation. He used the fact that I hardly had any contact with my family, and I couldn't see them because I got moved from placement to placement and never got settled enough to be allowed to see my family.

He would listen, and tell me, 'They don't care about you. They never came and got you.' Again, I was eighteen. My oldest sister is ten years older than me. It got me thinking: *she's an adult. Why didn't she come get me? Why didn't they care enough?* That made it easy for me to just stop talking to them altogether. Whatever little contact I did have, I stopped talking to them because he'd gotten inside my head. I'd think of my family, and I was convinced: *No. You didn't care.*

He would come back to LA, and we'd go out. I'm head over heels. He would take me to the mall and buy me shoes and a couple of outfits. For a girl who grew up in placements and group homes, that's huge. Every time I had to leave somewhere I'd lose all of my stuff. Some resident would either take it or someone wouldn't bother to pack it.

I was done with school, and he asked, 'You want to come with me?' He was telling me that he loved me, and I wanted to believe him. He bought me a ticket, and we went to New York. He was sweet for about two months, taking me out and buying me things. Then one day, he says, 'My friend is looking at you. He likes you. He wants to see you. He's cool.'

Why did I say yes? I was afraid of disappointing my boyfriend. It was a fear of disappointing him. I was just in bliss. I was in a whole new environment. I wasn't in the group homes. I wasn't fighting. There's someone telling me that they love me. All this great stuff.

But I still didn't want to do it with his friend. I put up some resistance, and he locked me in a walk-in closet. No food, no water, no nothing. He beat me up, and his friend raped me.

His friend told me, 'You just better do what he says. You just do what he say you do.'

For a couple of weeks, it was with his friend. Then he wanted me to do it with another friend. And I was like, 'I don't want to do this with you. I don't want to share you. I don't want it to be like that.'

Then he came over to me, and he hit me. He backhanded me across the mouth. I remember thinking, like, *This is real. This is the shit you read in books, the trash novels on the Walmart shelves.*

After that, it was just fear. A state of fear. I'm scared. I didn't want to disappoint him. I didn't want to make him mad. What he'd said after he hit me was, 'Don't make me be that guy. I don't want to be that guy with you.'

So that automatically made me think, *It's my fault. I made him be that guy. I made him be angry. I made him hit me.* Given my group home experiences, physical abuse was not foreign to me. It never entered my head to think, *I'm calling the cops on you.* It was a sense of almost like, *Okay, there's something I've done here. Whatever I've done, I got to stop doing that to stop him wanting to hit me.* You just stop fighting.

He'd broken me, and I just complied. Whatever he asked me to do, I complied. He'd broken my spirit, and he had me. He could get me to do whatever he wanted me to do. But I'd never seen him exchange any money. What he'd tell me was, 'These are my friends, these are my friends.'

One day, he couldn't even tell me the guy's name. I said, 'The tall guy. What's his name?'

And he was like, 'What's his name?'

I got hit for that because I challenged him: 'You told me everybody's your friend, and you don't know his name?'

After that, the beatings became almost normal. He just stopped hitting my face.

He would throw me to the floor, kick me, and punch me in the boobs over and over. It was a lot of traumatic shit. I was getting my ass whipped nearly every day. He'd spit on me, he fractured my ribs, and broke my arm. It wasn't just physical either. I think my ultimate breaking point was when he told me, 'I set you up. You really think that I would bring you out here to love on you?'

I was so confused because I'm like, 'That's what you said.' Even though someone shows you something else, you still believe what they said.

■ ■ ■

I was completely alone. When he broke my arm, I remember going to the hospital, and he wouldn't let me talk for myself. *I* couldn't tell them my name. *He* would tell them my name. He told them that *I* slipped on black ice. That's how *I* broke my arm. That's how this happened.

My trust in the medical system is little-to-none because I'm like, *You cannot* not *see this? You can't* not *see what's happening here.* I had spiral fracture of the left arm from where he twisted my arm and bent it behind my back. The doctor looks at the X-ray and asks, 'How did you twist your arm like that?'

I said, 'I fell.'

The doctor is looking at me; she's looking at him; she's looking at me. The doctor said, 'That's really strange because the bone is badly twisted. How did you do that?'

All I could say was, 'I fell.'

And the doctor didn't ask any more questions.

By the end of the first year, my boyfriend started taking me to Vegas and Miami for things like the Super Bowl weekend and spring break—high tourist times. He would have these pre-planned buyers lined up, and a hotel room booked. I didn't get to go out, and I didn't get to see anybody but the buyers. He was also selling the pills that the doctors would prescribe me for the pain. He's telling me I can't smoke. I can't drink. I can't do anything. 'Nobody wants to have sex with a drunk. Nobody wants to have sex with a person who's high.' So through it all, I was cognizant of everything, everything that was going on.

It was so bad I got suicidal. I started cutting on myself. The blood would flow, and I would feel better. I can't explain that. I just felt better. Other times, I tried to ingest whatever pills I could find around the house. He'd find me and take me to hospital to have my stomach pumped. They'd ask, 'Why did you do that? Why did you try to overdose?' He would tell them that it was an accident, that I didn't know my own tolerance.

I would get out of the hospital, and he would beat me up. He'd scream at me, 'You're putting everything at risk. Why are you being so stupid?' One time he choked me until I passed out. I remember him saying before everything went black, 'If you want to die, I'll kill you. You don't have to kill yourself. I'll kill you.'

My last suicide attempt, I just ran into the middle of traffic. I wanted to be hit by a car. If I cut myself, I'm not dying. If I try overdosing, I'm not dying. If he chokes me, I'm not dying. A car should kill me. But he ran out into the road with me. He grabbed me by the head with his hand under the back of my hair and he's holding it, and he's telling everybody, 'She's my sister! She's crazy! She's crazy!' And he's whispering to me, 'I'm going to kill you. *I'm* going to kill you.'

I told him, 'Just kill me right now. This is it. I'm out of here.'

He dragged me back into the car and told me I was a liability. He dropped me off at a bus stop in the dead of winter. New York City, in the dead of winter. All I had on was a t-shirt that was a little bit above my knees, and flip-flops. I didn't know anybody. I didn't have a phone. Early on, he took my phone. He told me I could use his, that I didn't have to have one of my own. I had no access to anyone out there.

An off-duty police officer stopped and asked, 'What are you doing out here?'

I said, 'I don't know.'

He was looking at all my bruises and scratches and the marks from cutting on myself. He said, 'Let me get you some help.' But there was no way I was getting in his car. He called the EMS,[7] and they took me to hospital. He came too, to make sure I was okay. I later learned the reason he stopped was not just because of his duty and oath, but because I reminded him of his daughter. That officer saw the human in me when I didn't see it in myself. When no one else did.

The officer asked me, 'Do you have somebody I can call? I'm going to try and find somebody.'

I told him my sister's name, and somehow they found her in California and arranged for me to go live with her. I was with my sister for two years, but I didn't speak. I was just numb. The system required 'victims of crimes' to get therapy, but I couldn't wrap my mind around all the times I wanted help but didn't get it. I didn't go to therapy, because I was convinced that they didn't care about me. For two years, I just didn't do anything.

But there came a point where I wanted to get out of the house. I wanted to do something. I just wanted to feel better. So I started going to school. I met some cool people in my classes who happened to have been through some equally messed-up stuff. Hearing their stories, it caused a shift in my mind. I didn't want to be *that* girl. Their stories, and the statistics I was reading about—it made me feel, *I don't want to be a statistic. I don't want to fall into the 70 percent category.* I was reading that 70 percent of all emancipated foster care youth end up homeless, and 63 percent of them end up in human sex trafficking.

There were no survivor numbers. Nothing else after that. No happy endings. No nothing. I wanted it to be something different. I read those numbers, and I thought, *I can't live like this forever. I can't wallow in my own shit.* I made some stupid decisions as far as thinking that I could just waltz my ass from California to New York and start living with someone I didn't know. I think that's the hardest part—forgiving yourself—forgiving yourself for being naïve. I was really young, really lonely, and hurt and broken, and once I owned it, I started to think about a future. I started to work on my relationship with my family. I was the one who had cut them off, but because I was doing better with myself, I started trying to bridge things with them.

It was hard talking to my sister because she didn't know what human trafficking was. *I* didn't know what human trafficking was! I didn't know it had a name for it. I didn't know I was a victim of something. All I knew was I had a crazy-assed boyfriend. I didn't know he was getting paid for my services until towards the end. There were a lot of things I didn't know until I got the help I needed. Talking to my sister was the beginning.

Then, it was a woman named Mary who was a huge part of my recovery. She founded the Long Beach Diversion Program, and she was running human trafficking support meetings. I'd never been with a group of like-minded people before. When I'd try to tell my sister what had happened, she couldn't understand it. Nobody understands it. Nobody's going to understand why you let somebody beat on you—what it was that made you stay or why you begin to have sex with someone's friend. Nobody understands what kind of mental state you have to be in to make you want to kill yourself. But like-minded people did. I started attending Mary's group, and everything changed.

But it wasn't easy. One night, one of the members was laughing during the class, and I asked her, 'Can you be quiet?' She threw coffee at me. I was ready to kick off.

Mary's like, 'Calm down, calm down, calm down.'

I was getting ready to leave. I said, 'I don't need this crap. I'm not cut out for this. I've been through way too much to go to a support group where people throw coffee at me.' As I got up to leave, the other girls got up to leave with me.

Mary came outside to talk with me. She said, 'I'm going to remove the girl that threw the coffee at you. Can you just come back inside?'

I go back inside, and the other five girls follow me.

After the meeting, Mary said to me, 'Tangelia, do you know you have power? You have the power to sway people, to move people. You lead people.' From there on she set me up with things to do. Soon I'm leading the group. She set me up with speaking gigs on human trafficking. And that's what I've been doing ever since.

■ ■ ■

I now go to the Long Beach Human Trafficking Task Force meetings. I tell them what to look for. I've been to medical conferences, and I tell them the telltale signs. Signs like my anxiety. How I avoided eye contact out of fear. The makeup covering my bruises. How I was unable to speak for myself— and my 'boyfriend's' unrealistic stories for my injuries. I tell them about the doctor who treated my spiral fracture. She just kept looking at me like, 'Are you going to say something?' And I'm just waiting for her to do something. We had this moment where we're just staring at each other. If she had said, 'I can't let you leave right now. Just wait here,' I could've been out of the game in six months. If only that doctor had said, 'This doesn't look right; this doesn't feel right.'

Especially at the medical conferences, I tell them, 'If someone acted on their gut and said, "I'm not going to let this girl leave here," my life could have been so different. Your intuition tells you everything. Trust your gut.'

I'm living proof that there is hope and life after even the worst of things. My hope is to help people see the signs and signals, before it's too late.

Tangelia is a human sex trafficking advocate and works with the organization, Gems Uncovered. Their mission statement is to "aid in rebuilding the lives of those affected by human trafficking and sexual exploitation, offering resources, counseling, awareness and education in a safe nurturing environment." Gems' goal is to "activate a healthy confidence within all survivors and equip each one with tools to soar past the pain and into their dreams with purpose. Gems turns victims into survivors by putting the human back into humanity."

gemsuncovered.org

5

A BETTER LIFE IN AMERICA?

The world has not even begun to fathom the devastating implications of a simple, straightforward statement buried in a little-known but thorough report by the United Nations which states: "Most poor people do not live under the shelter of the law, but far from the law's protection." There are at least 2.5 billion very poor people in the world ... [and put] simply: they are not safe. They are—by the hundreds of millions—threatened every day with being enslaved, imprisoned, beaten, raped, and robbed. ... The relentless threat of violence is part of the core subtext of their lives.[1]

GARY HAUGEN

On October 23, 2019, thirty-nine people were discovered dead in a container in Essex, England. The bodies were so closely packed together, the first policeman on the scene could not check them all for signs of life.[2] They had been locked in the back of a truck, suffering hyperthermia in the unbearable heat—estimated at 38.5°C (over 100°F). Forensic experts calculated the air in the trailer would have turned fatally toxic in nine hours. The victims were sealed in their truck-tomb for twelve. Ten teenagers were among the dead. All the victims were Vietnamese nationals, aged between fifteen and forty-four.

At the inquiry, the prosecutor explained to jurors what went wrong. "You may well conclude that on this occasion the criminals just got too greedy at £10,000 [$13,000] a head. They had too many people loaded into a single lorry."[3]

What follows is the story of a young woman who was a few short hours from a similar fate. Noemi's mother tongue is Akatek, a Guatemalan dialect. Her second language is Spanish. English is Noemi's third language. The transcription of her story has been rendered to make it more easily accessible to the reader.

■ ■ ■

I GREW UP IN POVERTY in Guatemala, nine hours away from Guatemala City. I lived in a house with four siblings—I'm the second oldest. We didn't really have a lot to eat, and there was not a lot of clothes.

My dad decided I should go to school, but my mom was

like, 'She's a girl. She's not supposed to be in school. She's supposed to be in the kitchen cooking for her brothers and sisters.'

My dad said, 'She needs to go to school,' so I went to school.

My mom was really mad and became abusive. Like, if I don't do anything around the house, she would beat me up. In the village where we lived, there's a lot of gossip that goes around. Mom would hear lies about me, and she'd beat me up. I didn't really have a good relationship with my parents—I never called them 'Mom' and 'Dad.' It was my grandma who was always there for me. She took care of me most of the time.

One day, my mom decided to send me to America. She said that in America I'd have a better life. In Guatemala we don't really celebrate birthdays, so I didn't know how old I was back then, but I was a young teenager. She contacted a smuggler in Guatemala to bring me to Mexico. I don't know where in Mexico because then I only spoke a little bit of Spanish—we spoke Akatek in my village—so there was so much I didn't understand. I didn't know where I was, or what was going to happen to me and the other people the smugglers were taking to Mexico.

We got close to the Guatemalan-Mexican border and had to walk through the mountains. We were stopped by thieves, and a lot of people I was with got beat up. The thieves stole our money and our food that we were carrying with us. The smugglers didn't protect us. After we were robbed, we had to keep going. We only walked when the sun went down because it was harder for Immigration to spot us. It was really scary; you can hear wild animals at night. The temperature was really, really hot, and I ran out of water. I just knelt down, and I told myself that I wouldn't make it to the United States because I was too weak. My feet were really sore because we had to walk, walk, walk. It's then that I cried out to God.

I looked up in the sky and asked God, 'If you're there, why did you create me? Why am I here on the earth? Like, I don't understand, you know?'

I think I passed out—I hadn't had food or water for days—but I felt like God spoke to me. He said, 'I did create you, and I created you for a purpose. You can make it. Keep going.'

Somehow that got me through. We crossed the border and were passed on to a different smuggler. We were put into the back of a tractor trailer, about a hundred of us. There was no room to sit. We had to stand up the whole time. It was really smelly. I had to keep my hand over my nose and tell myself just to keep breathing. It was terrifying. That whole time—about a week—it's a blur, partly because of the heat, partly because we weren't given anything to eat or drink, and partly because we were exhausted. I was so scared. The smugglers kept moving us in and out of trucks, and made us walk long distances over and over. I do remember spending a few days in Phoenix. They fed us just a little Mexican soup. It was so spicy, I could hardly eat it. Then another smuggler took me and one other immigrant to North Carolina. We drove all night and all day.

■ ■ ■

They split me and the other immigrant up, and even though we were in North Carolina, I started working for a Guatemalan man. I didn't get paid. I was like a slave. I worked for him for two and a half years. I did laundry and cooked. I was almost never allowed to leave the house. I asked him if I could go to school, and he would tell me that I'm not smart enough to go to school. He said, 'You are nothing. You are here to work for me, not go to school.' I had to get up early in the morning and make sure his kids were up in time to go to school. I had to look after the neighbor's kids as well—six kids I was taking care of. The oldest son, he was really abusive, and he'd beat me up with a broomstick. He'd tell me that I was really, really stupid, that I didn't know anything. At that time, I hardly spoke any English, so I couldn't talk to him. He'd just beat me, over and over and over again.

One day I decided to run away. I didn't have any idea where I was going. I packed up my clothes in a Walmart bag, and I went to this Mexican store near us. By then, my Spanish was good enough that I could ask the lady for help. But she didn't help me. There was this other Mexican lady who walked into the store, and she saw me crying.

She asked me what was wrong, and I told her. She said that I could come to her house. But the man I worked for found out I was gone, and he went looking for me. He ended up going to the Mexican store because he knew I used to go there to get groceries. The lady from the Mexican store told him I went with this other lady, and he found out her address. He came to her house, and when he saw me, he grabbed me by my hair and pulled me into his van and took me back to his house. When we got there, he dragged me into the house and beat me with his belt. He kicked me several times and told me that I was never, ever to run away again.

I stayed another year, and I didn't try to escape anymore because I was scared. He continued to beat me, and then he started raping me. He was telling me that we should move to New York and start a family. I would tell him, 'You have a wife, you have kids,' but he tried to convince me to go live with him somewhere else.

One Sunday morning his wife was at church, and I stayed behind with the kids. He also stayed home that morning, and he started to beat me and rape me again. That Sunday morning, I tried to fight him back. He had left the door open, and I could escape. I started running—out through the yard and into the woods. He was chasing me and screaming at me.

I ran through the woods to a neighbor's house. I was shaking, and I couldn't speak. I finally caught my breath and was able to tell her, 'Someone is chasing me.' They called the police. The man was taken to jail, and I was taken to the hospital. I stayed in hospital for a few days, and they had to find a foster family for me. They didn't know what to do with me because I didn't speak hardly any English and only a little Spanish back then. Finally, they found a woman named Jeni—she speaks Spanish, and they were able to place me with her."

■ ■ ■

Noemi's foster mom, Jeni, interjected at that point.

"Noemi had a rape kit examination done at the hospital and that was proof of what had happened. However, she didn't have any identification or documents that stated her age. When her case went to court, the opposing side presented a birth certificate. The District Attorney told us that it was very easy to get fake documents from Guatemala. A lot was riding on her age—because in North Carolina, when you rape a sixteen-year-old, the consequences are a lot smaller than if she had been under sixteen. I think she was probably thirteen or fourteen at the time. They were saying she was sixteen.

The man was eventually convicted of statutory rape and was incarcerated for four years—the minimum sentence for raping a sixteen-year-old. He was then deported back to Guatemala. We think he was a distant cousin to someone in Noemi's family. That was the Guatemalan connection.

This was 2010. I believe Noemi was the first human trafficking case in our local community. People didn't know what to do or how to prosecute these things. It was her word against his word. The court *did* know that there was no record of any medical care given to Noemi prior to the rape, and that she was not put in school. The family got food stamps, and she wasn't counted as someone in the household. She was kept secret. Even though the courts knew all this, they certainly didn't prosecute to the full extent of the law.

Poor Noemi. Once she was in foster care, we had legal aid of North Carolina coming to interview her. She had law enforcement officers and social workers and attorneys wanting to talk to her, but she spoke no English. She didn't know the word 'hello' when she came to my home. Her Spanish was broken. I have a Bachelor's degree in Spanish, but I'm not 100 percent fluent. We communicated in broken Spanish and hand gestures for quite a while.

Once we got through the court case, she was thrown into the ninth grade here—even though social services assessed her level of education as kindergarten. She could read a little, and she could write, but crudely. But she knew no math. She didn't know how to add. Didn't know what one plus three was! But she had some amazing, very inspirational ESL [English as a Second Language] teachers. They watched over her like she was their daughter. They knew her story, and were so very kind to her. They patiently taught her English.

We were terrified to throw her into American high school with the kind of kids that are there. She hated it the first year and a half."

■ ■ ■

Noemi took over her story.

"I still couldn't speak English. I'd go to class, but I didn't understand what my teachers were saying. I didn't even know if they were asking me questions. I certainly couldn't answer. A lot of kids made fun of me because I didn't speak English, and I felt so alone in high school. I'd eat my lunch in the bathroom by myself and just cry.

At night I would have terrible, horrible nightmares. They were so bad I was afraid of going to sleep. During the day I would remember some segment from my childhood, and I would get so sad that I didn't want to live anymore. There were times I'd hurt myself. Everybody had told me I was just trash, and I was believing them. Nobody wanted me in Guatemala, and I didn't want to be in America. I felt like I'd rather be dead than live in this world. Since then, I've had a lot of therapy, and I know now that once the abuse stops, once you're out of survival mode, everything comes crashing in. That's why I was so tormented by memories of what had happened to me.

■ ■ ■

In freshman year, I joined track and field, and that's what got me through my high school years. I was only just learning English, so I had to communicate with my coaches through my hands. I wasn't very good—any race I was in, I'd come in last, but I just kept running. By my senior year I moved up to fourth place on the girls cross country team. Running saved my life. When I ran away from the man who was raping me, I ran over a mile through the woods—barefoot. Back in Guatemala, I would run away after my mother would beat me. I would run when other kids would try to beat me up. And running has been a big part of my therapy.

■ ■ ■

I wanted to go to school my whole life. When I finally got in school, I couldn't believe the way the American students treated their teachers. They didn't appreciate that they were getting a free education. Where I came from, there's not a lot of kids who go to school 'cause Guatemala is a poor country. I really wanted to go to school and have the opportunity to be somebody and not get married at the age of fourteen and start having babies. Here in America, everybody has the freedom to go to school. But the students were really disrespectful to their teachers. That made me upset because I wish that I was born here and had the privilege of education. In high school, it seemed everybody complained about their teachers, complained about their lives. It didn't seem like they appreciated any of the things that they have.

In May 2020, Noemi graduated from Gardner-Webb University with a Bachelor's degree in Criminal Justice and a minor in Homeland Security. She has now also been granted US citizenship and has started her first job in her career field.

THIS IS ALL I'M GOOD FOR

Women in prostitution do not wake up one day and "choose" to be prostitutes. It is chosen for us by poverty, past sexual abuse, the pimps who take advantage of our vulnerabilities, and the men who buy us for the sex of prostitution.[1]

MANIFESTO, COALITION AGAINST TRAFFICKING IN WOMEN CONFERENCE, 2005

When you are fifteen years old and destitute, too unskilled to work and too young to claim unemployment benefit, your body is all you have left to sell.[2]

RACHEL MORAN, SURVIVOR

Sam grew up in a family that moved around a lot. Her dad worked for a multinational company—so she was born in the UK, but when she was four years old her family moved to Australia where she went to primary and middle school. Her family was then relocated to New Zealand after she'd started high school.

■ ■ ■

IT WASN'T ALWAYS THE EASIEST to adjust. I had a supportive family, but they were busy working parents, and with all the moves I definitely needed more stability, and so I grew up to be a shy, quiet child who loved to read. My family is Hindu background, and that made fitting in at school even more difficult. I was not a happy teenager, and I tried to commit suicide, but it didn't go very well. That made me feel even worse because I thought, *Good Lord, I can't even do that right.*

Indian culture treats mental health challenges as shameful, and trying to commit suicide certainly brought shame on my parents. They tried taking me to a therapist, but that didn't work out because I felt like the therapist didn't really understand why I was so upset. I decided to run away from home, and because I finished the 10th grade year, I had my school certificate. In New Zealand that meant you can go to work. I hit the streets looking for a job. I found one, in what I thought was a nightclub. Given how quickly they hired me, I should have known something was wrong. I was desperate, so I didn't think it through very well. I was only sixteen.

I showed up for work that first day thinking, *Oh my gosh, it's so easy to get a job. This is amazing.* They put me to work at the front desk, and I did think it was a little odd, all these women wandering around in ball gowns everywhere, and it did seem weird that the only people coming through the door were guys. But then I'd never been to a nightclub, so I didn't know what it was meant to look like. At the end of the night, the manager said to me, 'There's something wrong with the take on the till. Can you come upstairs to fix it?' If I'd had any sense of what to look out for, red flags would have been going off in every direction, but I didn't know any better.

He took me upstairs, and as soon as I got up there, I realized I was in trouble. But it was too late. He locked me in a room, and that was pretty much that. In the beginning I fought anybody who'd come near me. I wouldn't eat. I wouldn't do anything. But you quickly realize that compliance is easier than fighting because you just lose hope after a little while. There's only so many beatings you can endure. You can only go so long without food or water. And they're either going to rape you or you can pretend that you're willing. I just got to the point where I decided that compliance meant that at least I'd survive. I worked at becoming numb, thinking, *I guess this is my life.*

I ended up there for nine months. One of my customers realized after a few visits that I really didn't want to be doing what I was doing. He started explaining to me ways to try to leave. The best way was to be more compliant. He'd say, 'The more you win them over, the more freedom you'll have. Once they let you out by yourself, we'll be able to help you.'

And so, little by little, I won the confidence of the different people who were in charge. The better I treated the customers, and the more compliant I was with their wishes, the more I earned different privileges, like choosing what you wanted to eat or being able to go out with the other girls. Someone always had their eye on us, but over time I earned the right to go down to the corner shop by myself.

Once I was allowed out on my own, that was when my john came and got me. He took me to a Christian shelter for vulnerable women. But I didn't know how to survive out in society. I felt completely useless. I tried to get a job, and things went from bad to worse. I got a job selling encyclopedias door-to-door.

We'd get driven around to all different parts of the country, and we'd knock on doors for hours a day. Our employer would feed us, and pile us into cheap hotel rooms, but somehow we never got paid. It didn't take long for me to say, 'Oh my God, this sucks so bad.'

Not long into the gig, I shoplifted an eyebrow pencil from the local Woolworths. I got arrested, and you could say that there were pros and cons to this. I got sent to jail because I didn't have a home. I didn't have an address. I was underage, and they figured I was a flight risk. I spent a week or so in jail, and of course I was terrified, but the women in prison actually understood what I had gone through. They understood because they had been through similar things. And three meals a day and a warm bed—that's not the worst thing in the world. They kept me in jail until they could find me a probation officer.

Now I was out of jail, but I was still homeless, and I was without a job. My probation officer was telling me, 'You've got to find a job.' What-the-freak kind of job did she want me to do? I was seventeen. I have an arrest record, no education, and I don't exactly have an employment record that's going to impress anybody. 'Find a job.' All right. So … onward to the massage parlor where, again, I started as a front desk person.

And very quickly, I realized this is not the normal kind of massage parlor. But at this point I'm over it. I was like, *All right, whatever. This is apparently my life, and this is all I'm good for, and this is all I can do.*

So ... brothel life, here we come. The lady who ran it, honestly, she wasn't that bad. She wasn't mean, and they didn't beat us. She let us keep 50 percent of what we earned. That meant I actually had a paycheck that I could take to probation to show them that I had a real job, and that meant I didn't get thrown in jail again. So I was thinking, *Alright, this isn't the worst thing in the world.* It almost felt like a real job. I worked both the front desk and the back rooms, and if probation was coming to check on me, I was out front, and it looked like a nice, decent massage place.

I saved enough money to rent a room from a disabled lady. She was very sweet to me and tried to help me in all sorts of ways. But I was just in survival mode at that point, and the only thing I cared about was me. One of my customers at the massage parlor asked me what I needed, and I told him that I really needed to figure out how to buy a vehicle because I wasn't eighteen yet. For obvious reasons, nobody's going to sell me a car. He cooked up this great idea that I steal my landlady's checkbook, and we'd go buy a car.

Less than a good idea. I told him I couldn't do that. Et cetera, et cetera. He said, 'What you're doing here is illegal, right? So what's one more step?'

And I was like, 'No, no, she's a really nice lady, and she's disabled.'

He said, 'Let me help you out. Either you do this or I'm going to kill you.'

I was terrified. I was thinking, *Who do you tell this to?* I mean, who's gonna believe you if you tell them? So I went ahead and did it. I stole the checkbook, and he and I went and bought the car.

I'm a terrible driver. The next day I totaled the car, but I was okay. The police reported the accident to my probation officer; my parents were called, and they took care of everything, and we settled out of court. But my parents couldn't figure out what to do with me. I'll give the probation lady this: she definitely helped my parents get me to a different environment. I was sent to live with my grandma in West Virginia and finish high school. But nobody's talking about the trauma I've endured. Certainly, nobody's treating it. Everybody thinks I should just be able to work through it.

■ ■ ■

I graduated from high school, and I wanted to be a chef, so I went off to a state culinary institute. As part of the course, I had to do practical hours, so I started working at a very exclusive club, and I made the mistake of telling my story to the folks in the kitchen. It literally didn't even take two days before I was told that I won't be able to continue school unless I start servicing their clientele. And off we go. We're back in the cycle. Once again, this is my life.

I grew up Hindu, and it's all about what you do. You have to earn your way through life. Karma kicks in, and everything gets sorted out in reincarnation. In my world, I knew that I would be coming back as a worm next time, or something worse. I was definitely not moving up the food chain any time soon. I was definitely going down.

Things go from bad to worse. I was run by a cartel down in the south-east, and they dragged me from the Super Bowl to the next big party. I was living in cars and planes and trains, and moved from city to city. I'm Sri Lankan, and there are not a lot of us for sale in the United States, so I had a high street value. We're not talking about a brothel situation anymore. Now it's high-end hotels and all-night work. I was sold for a day, a week, a month, and with the high-end party scene, there was a lot of drugs. My drug of choice was cocaine. Coke helped me cope. And if you weren't 'in the mood,' we were made to take ecstasy.

After one Super Bowl weekend, I was so tired. I told my handlers, 'I just want out. I want a normal life. I want to go back to school.'

They're like, 'Out? What is *that*? Absolutely not. *This* is your life. This is what you do, and this is how you do it.' Obviously, the conversation did not go as I had hoped.

They decided to open new offices in West Palm Beach. They were pleased with the work I was doing, and so they promoted me. They told me I wouldn't have to do as much work if I started recruiting other women for the new office. I figured that was better than nothing. I still wanted to leave, so I started squirreling away the part of the money that I was allowed to keep, and I continued to do whatever they wanted me to do 'cause I didn't want any problems. That didn't last long because they found out that I was making plans to leave, and they literally beat me within an inch of my life.

My cheekbones were shattered, my face was all cut up, and I was unrecognizable. I didn't know what to do. I hadn't talked to my family in years, but I decided to take a chance and called my grandma. I told her that I'd been mugged. My aunt bought me a plane ticket back to West Virginia, and I looked so ridiculously horrible, I'm shocked they let me on the plane.

When I was sent to West Virginia from New Zealand, the high school I attended was run by a church, and everybody in the church had been unbelievably nice to me. They showed me the love of God in a way I had never experienced before. The high school principal was really kind too. When I returned, she knew something was up, but I wasn't in a place to tell her or anyone my story.

Once I'd recovered a bit from the beating, I went back to church, and one of the ladies looked at me and knew something in the whole mugging story was not right. She told my uncle that she'd drive me home after church. She then got our pastor's wife alongside. She's a psychologist, and she listened to me tell my story about being mugged, and then she said, 'I've seen this before. I need you to tell us what really happened here because there's a lot that doesn't make sense.' I opened up and told them everything. They were amazing. They said, 'It's all right; we're going to take care of you. We're going to help you.'

They drove me back to my aunt and uncle's house and explained to them what had really happened and what was going on. Once they left, my aunt then had a complete meltdown and kicked me out of the house 'cause she's like, 'You're going to be a horrible influence on our kids; you've brought all this danger here, and you've got to leave now.'

I called the church, and my high school principal came and got me, and I lived with her for a while. Things were going really well. I got a job as a waitress in a restaurant. I didn't have any bank accounts or credit cards in my name, so no one could find me—the church was very particular about that. I was getting some therapy, and I eventually applied to go to college. I'm like, *Okay, it's getting better. Things are getting better.*

I moved on campus, but I still hadn't worked through all of the trauma. And around college campuses, who's prowling in the shadows? Recruiters, right? And who do they go after? The vulnerable. Here we go round the merry-go-round. I did a semester of college, but I hadn't learned my lesson about not sharing my story. Come spring break, my new friends said, 'Let's go on a road trip to Texas.'

■ ■ ■

I didn't come back from Texas because these new friends had connected all the dots, and now I was back in the game again. At that point, I had just given up and given into the fact that this was my life. It wasn't hard to control me because I literally didn't think I was good for anything else.

I worked in Texas for a few months, and then they wanted me to move up to Chicago. They convinced me to go because they said I could go to school up there. I figured, *Okay. I'm going to work my way through school, and things are going to get better.* But they don't. Shockingly, they don't.

I was now in a different league. It's the really high-end customers. It's big Chicago dollars, servicing politicians and actors. At the time, I was staying in a hotel, and I was really cranky and upset. By now, there was more than enough proof that this is apparently my life, and that's it. That's all. This is all we're ever going to have. One morning, there's all this noise coming from next door, and I left my room, more or less to yell at them because I was so annoyed that it's early and they're making all this noise. But it's a church, and they've rented the hotel 'cause it's Sunday morning. I can't really explain why, but I felt compelled to stay for the service. This will date me, but at the time, I had one of those giant brick phones that I had to carry around with me. That was how my handlers gave me my orders. I was sitting at the back of the church, and the pastor was preaching about how God calls you—and my bloody phone starts ringing!

Everybody in church turns right around and stares at me. I'm like, *Holy crap*! I didn't know what to do. I thought that getting up and leaving would just make things worse. So I sat there and listened to the message. It was all about God calling us to do things that he created us to do. I didn't have a clue what God wanted me to do, but I did start going to church regularly—but with one foot in and one foot out.

I started paying tithes with the illicitly gotten gains of my life. I was giving the church 10 percent of the money I was making in the game. I started reading my Bible, and I was feeling more and more conviction about what I was doing. And the more involved I got at church, the less I wanted to go to work. During this time, one of my handlers got killed. He was the mean one of the two, and once he was dead, the other one was willing to negotiate a way that I could pay him off for my freedom.

Finally, I didn't have someone handling me, but I still didn't know what to do. Then I had a dream: I'm supposed to help other girls get out. In the dream, I bought a house, and we all live in it together. I figured that the dream was from God, but I told him, 'I don't know how to do that. Let me try this instead. Let me become a madam. I'll treat my girls *so* good. I'll give them 90 percent of their money, and I'll help them go to school, and we're all going to be Kumbaya together.' Well, that went totally wrong. I got some other folks together, and we were good business people. We eventually expanded things, so that we were operating brothels in thirty-three States. We were nice to our girls, but that didn't really matter because it wasn't the way to solve their problems.

Or mine. I got arrested and ended up with a felony conviction for wire fraud because that's all the authorities could actually prove. But it took years for this to go to trial. By this point, I was married, I had a daughter, and I'm working a good, honest job— then, all of a sudden, it was off to federal prison. Seven months later, I was sent back to the UK because I wasn't a US citizen. My husband and daughter moved to the UK, and I started working in technology. It wasn't long before I recognized that the grooming and recruitment of girls was significantly online.

I started volunteering on a project called ProNino. Its mission was to curtail child trafficking, and we worked in thirteen Spanish-speaking countries. While selling software to investment companies, I realized that I actually had a way to help stop the trafficking of children—because of my tech work and my knowledge of the dark web—and I could do that work and still stay behind the scenes. Nobody had to know my story. I could just work away and quietly execute.

As I was working online, I was seeing that we could do outreach, we could work with vulnerable women, and we could connect the dots on some of the networks. We could analyze where the women were coming from and where they were going. So much of the traffic comes up through Africa and across into Spain. And they're using some pretty crazy techniques. Many of the women aren't just being trafficked; they're being used as drug mules as well. Instead of silicone breast implants, they're implanted with heroin-filled implants. Once they get to Spain, their breasts are cut open and they're left disfigured, and because prostitution is legal in Spain, they're put to work on the streets. Everything these women were promised back in Africa doesn't exist. It's the same for families in South American countries who were promised money for selling their girls—often $20,000—with the promise of another $20,000 when they get to their final destination. On arrival, the girls are told that their families would be killed if they didn't comply. They never see the money.

■ ■ ■

My husband and my daughter really wanted to move back to the US, and, after a long wait, the Embassy finally granted us our visas. That meant that my daughter could go to high school in the US, so she was super happy. I still wanted to continue the ProNino work, so I commuted back and forth to Europe. My company was supportive, though a lot of people wondered why I was so passionate about this issue. I'd just shrug; 'Some people are passionate about animals; some people are passionate about water. I'm passionate about human trafficking.' I'm still not explaining when and how and why.

Then my husband and I began serving at Willow Creek Community Church as section pastors. They already had an anti-human trafficking ministry, and as I got more and more involved there, I was asked about the work I was doing and how I got into it. Obviously, the senior staff at Willow knew about my past, and it was in my HR record, but at that time we were only telling people who needed to know about my past and my criminal record. But some of the leadership team were encouraging me to tell some of my story, and I told them that they were out of their minds. I was not going to do that. I had a great life. I had the stability I'd always wanted. I have a loving husband. I have a child. I have a good job. I have a house. I'm not interested in reliving my past, but thanks for asking.

They respected that, but asked if they could just videotape a few interviews. They said they didn't ever have to use them, but it might be helpful to see what impact my story might have. Again, I told them they were out of their minds, but I said I'd try. I couldn't get through a single session without breaking down. I couldn't do it. They quickly figured out that I wasn't ready because I was reliving too much of it. And I realized I needed to go back to therapy.

My therapist is a super cool woman of faith who knew what I'd been through. She assured me that the telling of my story would make an impact, and I said that I couldn't get through it without breaking down, so I didn't think it was a good thing. She suggested that we pray about it. Every day, before the therapy session started, we'd pray. Over the next decade, my therapist helped me come to a broader understanding of what led me into trafficking, how it happened, and what parts I can own, and what parts I don't need to own. I had done Beth Moore's *Breaking Free* course,[3] so I had a head knowledge about my trauma, and through the therapy, the healing went so much deeper. Today we teach *Ending the Game*,[4] which is a curriculum co-authored by Rachel Thomas. It helps women understand the psychological trauma of being trafficked and how to stop the cycle.

But telling my story publicly still didn't seem like a good idea. However ... we organized a singles event at the church and 1,500 people were registered. My husband—the one trained as a pastor, the one who is an orator—was scheduled to speak. But his plane gets delayed. He's stuck in Denver. We tried to figure out what to do, and somebody suggested that he email his talk to me, and I could deliver it. I was thinking that everybody had seriously lost their minds, but I stood up ... and I instantly knew I couldn't deliver his speech—because it's not mine. Instead, I just started talking, and I am absolutely certain that the Holy Spirit took over because in my right mind, I would never have done that.

The whole story comes out. My daughter was in the audience; my mother-in-law was there; all my friends were there in the first few rows, as well as a whole ton of people. My daughter and my mother-in-law and some of my friends only knew pieces of the puzzle, but that night I emptied out the whole box. At the end of the talk, I felt this amazing sense of peace, like all the things that I had been afraid of suddenly didn't matter. It was an extremely freeing experience. But I can tell you, had anybody in a bazillion years told me that speaking was the plan for that Friday night, I would have laughed them off the stage!

It was just one of those God-moments. I couldn't have prepared it—except that I had been preparing it with the pastors for the videos they tried to record. That night I felt supported and loved and enabled. People understood *why* I was so passionate about human trafficking, and some of them got inspired. I did too. I still wanted to provide housing for vulnerable women—the fulfilment of the dream-vision that God had given me a decade and a half before. I was finally ready to do things in his way, and it was out of that talk that I went on to found Rahab's Daughters.

As an organization, Rahab's Daughters is now five years old, and we have four safe houses around the country that enable us to do a lot of prevention and rescue. And we were thrilled to host the first BRAVE event here in Chicago. I'm so amazed at the evaluations and the feedback from the girls. We had a number of survivors at the event as well, and they thought it was superb.

I'm so fortunate to be able to work for an IT corporation that fully supports what I do, and to be able to marry my passion and my job together. Had I not been transparent with folks in explaining my story, they wouldn't have understood why it was so important to me, and I think they would have been a lot less accommodating. It's been great being able to juggle these two things together, and it's been great because I get to spend time in corporate America, to go into the business world and do things and raise corporate awareness and support, and then I give back, as I get involved on the frontlines and work with vulnerable women. I'm not having vicarious trauma all the time, as I'm not working with survivors full-time. I get a bit of a break.

It's been really just amazing. God has orchestrated it so that I can balance the two worlds, and I feel like I'm making an impact. We still do a lot of work behind the scenes on technology and trafficking. It's one of the big pieces that we work on. But we've also been at the last seven Super Bowls on rescue missions. We know where to go and where to look and how to find the girls, and we're able to talk to them, and as we share our stories, they know that we know that it sucks to do the work. There's credibility when we tell them, 'You have a chance to do something different too if you want to.' We tell them that they have our support, and we're there for them. We share with them programs like *Ending the Game*—programs we use that are written by survivors.

On average, it takes seven to twelve times for someone to want to come out for good. To be able to say, 'Look, it took me four or five attempts, so, it's okay. It's not abnormal. It's hard, but it's definitely possible. There are different ways to go about it. Let's help you figure it out.' That's the really cool and amazing part of my life at this point. And I'm always thankful that I've been able to change the trajectory of my life in this way. And that's God, 100 percent.

7

AN EXPERIMENT
GONE WRONG

Incest is boot camp. Incest is where you send the girl to learn
how to do it. ... She's trained. And the training is specific
and it is important: not to have any real boundaries to her
own body; to know she's only valuable for sex. ... But even
that is not enough, because then she runs away and she
is out on the streets and homeless. For most women, some
version of all these kinds of destitution needs to occur.[1]

ANDREA DWORKIN

By the time Taanis was eleven, she was painfully aware she didn't belong—anywhere, to anyone.

She didn't understand prejudice, or racism, or cultural bias, but she did know it was her skin color that kept her from fitting in. Taanis came up with a creative solution. One evening she took a long bath *in bleach.* She figured if it worked on laundry, it would work on her. If she could bleach herself white, people wouldn't hate her. She'd be loved. She'd be accepted.

It didn't work.

It wasn't the only experiment that didn't work. For thirty years, starting in the late 1950s, an estimated twenty thousand Aboriginal Canadian children were taken from their birth families and fostered or adopted by white middle-class families, in what became known as "The Sixties Scoop." That benign name was later recognized as "systemic cultural genocide."[2] In an article titled "Identity Lost and Found: Lessons from the Sixties Scoop," Raven Sinclair succinctly put the Scoop in its broad context:

> The white social worker, following on the heels of the missionary, the priest and the Indian agent, was convinced that the only hope for the salvation of the Indian people lay in the removal of their children.[3]

Hope and salvation it was not.

Canada's Indigenous peoples comprise only 4 percent of the national population, yet more than 50 percent of all sex trafficking victims in Canada are

Indigenous. The reasons for this are complex but are ultimately rooted in a shameful legacy of poverty, racism, and abuse.[4] On February 14, 2017, Superior Court Justice Edward Belobaba ruled in favor of the class action suit on behalf of Indigenous children affected by the Sixties Scoop. In his ruling, he acknowledged that,

> the loss of their Aboriginal identity left the children fundamentally disoriented, with a reduced ability to lead healthy and fulfilling lives … resulting in psychiatric disorders, substance abuse, unemployment, violence and numerous suicides.[5]

Taanis was one of those children.

She is a Cree First Nations from Northern Alberta. Both her parents were addicts and alcoholics, and still are. When Taanis was two and a half years old, her grandmother found her and her three sisters in an abandoned house on the Reserve, tied up to chairs. Taanis' half-sister is four years older, and from a different tribe (the Blackfoots), and both girls were adopted by a single white woman.[6] The adoption agreement stipulated regular contact with their biological family.

■ ■ ■

I'D GET TO SEE MY family at least once a year. That was actually the highlight of the year because I was introduced to my aunts and uncles, and they'd spoil me! It was great because growing up at home with my half-sister, she'd always conform, be the good girl—so she was the one who got the treats, the attention. That's something I looked for my whole life—attention, identity, belonging, being heard, being valued—and my aunties would give me that.

But when I'd go back to the Reserve, it was also the times I'd be sexually assaulted. I didn't know it was assault—I was too young. I was told it was love. But I knew it wasn't right. My sister had gone through the same thing, and when I told her what was happening to me, she said it was okay ... that it was normal.

Normal.

I didn't know any better. It started when I was four and continued 'til I was seven.

My adopted mom and my biological grandmother instilled in me that 'You always need to be honest'; 'You need to respect your elders.' Those were my basic values.

When I went back to the Reserve, I always wondered who my mother and father were, but nobody would talk about them. I learned much later that the reason for the silence was that both my parents were addicts, and everybody knew they didn't want to take any responsibility for me or my sister.

We didn't have any kind of male role model growing up; it was just me, my sister, and my single stepmom. On the Reserve, my grandfather and my Uncle Johnny, they were as close as it got. I was a wild-child growing up, curious, and a tomboy—and they would teach me everything a dad would teach you. They'd take me out fishing, make Native dance—those were my favorite times. I loved it. But when I was seven, my sister and I got into a fight, and she told me that my uncle was actually my father.

I went into the house, and all my family was there, both my adopted and biological family. When I asked, 'Is Uncle

Johnny my dad?' the whole house went quiet. The silence was my answer. My whole world broke that day. I knew it was true and that everybody had lied to me. But I wanted it not to be true.

I ran out of the house and went next door to Uncle Johnny's. I pounded on the door, and when he answered it, I yelled, 'Are you my dad?'

He stopped talking to me that day. Not a word, 'til I was sixteen, when my grandmother died.

Everything I had known to be true, the most important people in my life—they'd lied to me. People that said they loved me and were supposed to be protecting me—they lied to me.

I literally remember giving the world the finger that day, and now when I look back on it, I put the little girl inside me to sleep. I built up all these walls so that no one could get in ... no one could hurt me.

■ ■ ■

My adopted mom was an amazing social activist, and she was so busy fighting for my people's rights, but me and my sister got lost in that shuffle. What me and my sister got was *stuff*—we got to go on trips, or I got a pair of skis—and that was how my mom showed us her love. That, and the message, 'Go out and be the best Cree Indian skier you can be.' I was on the ski team at Sunshine Mountain. For years, I trained hard, but I never fit in, and I was never good enough. I'd win a gold medal, and instead of hearing, 'I'm proud of you' from my mom, it was, 'You could have done better.' How could I have done better? I just won the gold medal!

I always felt that I was an experiment gone wrong.

Going back and forth from the Reserve and my biological family, to my mom's house with her university friends, I learned to adapt myself to whoever I was with. As I started getting older, I got a lot of attention when I did bad things. I got really good at doing bad things. I ended up in front of my first judge and landed in juvie hall when I was ten years old. I didn't like the detention center, except for one thing. My body was changing by the time I was eleven. I matured quite early on, and while I was in juvie, all these young boys were giving me attention. It felt like, finally, I *was* somebody, somebody that was loved, somebody that was wanted. I just didn't have any direction, anybody telling me, 'Hey, who you are is precious. Keep who you are—you're a gift. Don't just easily give yourself away.' I had learned just the opposite. Because I was abused as a young girl, I thought that's the way it worked—that my body was for a man's use.

Just before my twelfth birthday I was walking in my neighborhood, and a much older man picked me up, drove me outside the city limits, gave me some alcohol, and then proceeded to give me a crash course on blow jobs. Booze for blow jobs. That's how it worked.

It wasn't a month later that I went from one world to another. I ran away from home. Nobody wanted me; I was just a pain in everybody's butt, and I was always doing something wrong. I couldn't live up to my mom's expectations, no matter what I did.

I ended up on the streets of Calgary, and I was introduced to some street kids who accepted me. They pulled me in; it was like the family I'd always been looking for. It was tight. There was intimacy. There were hugs; there was, 'Hey, how are you doing? Where have you been? Are you hungry? Let's get you something to eat.' Someone would bring a guitar; someone would bring some weed; somebody brought food; and we all shared. It wasn't about money. It was about what we had to share. And I was *in*.

One of the things I could share was what I knew about the system. I had been in and out of trouble with the law, and I knew I could get away with pretty much anything because I was under eighteen and wouldn't be charged, as I was a minor. The new gang took advantage of that. I was doing things that were scary for me, things I thought I'd never do. I can always remember my whole life thinking, *This can't be it. There's got to be something more.*

My mom's life was all about money and status; where you were in society, and it was always, 'You get your own house, and then you can do what you want.' I wanted to conform, so I was led by that. I thought, *If I can get my own money, then I get to be my own boss.* That's what I heard. That's what was echoing round in my head.

One of my street-friends, Patsy, had a history I can't even begin to fathom. She had been sold as a little kid. Her mom used to sell her to her johns, and Patsy brought me into this whole new world. When I told her I needed to make some money, she said, 'I'm going to help you. I'll tell you how this works.' Some of the stuff she taught me was how to be careful. It was a survival thing. Like, she had given me a knife. When you're getting paid for your services, things can go really wrong. I learned that the hard way.

I got raped on the first 'date' I ever did. The guy took my knife away from me, and I thought he might even kill me. He didn't though; he just raped me and beat me up. I felt like that's the way I deserved to be treated. That's what life had shown me. That's what I believed I was worth. It really set in the shame. It screams at you; it literally screams at you. And it echoes what you've heard your whole life: *that's all you're good for.*

If somebody had been there to help me, somebody who would have walked me through all I was having to deal with, they would have helped me see that it's not just shame, but it's hurt and pain from my youth and my childhood. But when you don't know what's going on, it just turns into anger. Your survival skills just turn it into anger, to suppress it. I got into years of drug and alcohol abuse, but it wasn't to detach myself. I learned *that* at seven years old. I learned to detach myself because I had to—because trauma had become the norm.

A few months later … wrong place, wrong time. I got gang-raped just before I turned thirteen. It got me pregnant, and with nowhere else to go, I went back to my mom. I told her what had happened. She freaked out. Her response was that it was my fault because I had put myself in that position. But she said she'd 'fix it' for me. We went to Hawaii for Christmas, and while we were there, I had an abortion. We were with another family, and right after I had the abortion my mom made me go down to the pool with the other kids like everything was okay.

■ ■ ■

I didn't last long back at home. *You see me as nothing? I'll show you what nothing can do!* It was hard-core rebellion. Though I was only a young teenager, I was mean, I was angry; the people around me knew I was off, that I could go off in a second, and it earned me a bit of a reputation. I was 'adopted' into a bike gang in Calgary, and soon it wasn't unusual to be in the presence of a knife or a gun or a life-threatening situation—two or three times a day. I was going out with the sergeant of arms of the Rebels, and I thought that this might be my freedom, that this might be my pass. This might be the love ... but the guy was a hard-core addict. I knew being with him wasn't love, but it gave me a little break from trying to make it on the streets by myself.

It eventually got so bad—he got really abusive and violent—I had to run away. I then got in between two people you shouldn't get in between, and I got thrown out a two-story window. I got hurt really bad. I collapsed two discs in my back. My ex-boyfriend actually took me to the hospital, and while we were waiting on my X-rays, I told him, 'I'm never coming back.'

He said, 'I don't want you back. You're broken.'

The next thing I know, the doctors are telling me I probably wouldn't ever walk again. Not me. I walked out of hospital—with a Demerol and morphine addiction. About the same time, crack cocaine came on the scene, and things got really ugly. Literally within months. People started turning on each other.

Crack played a big part in changing the scene, but there were other things going on. Every week there were 'missing' posters going up. We were quite a tight-knit thing; we didn't have cell phones back then, but we knew what was going on. We'd touch base each night because women were going missing. There were psycho killers that were preying on prostituted women.

Vancouver was the most famous one—Robert Pickton, the pig farmer[7]—but it wasn't just there, and it wasn't just him. Literally, dozens and dozens and dozens of women disappeared. Women hitchhiking … never seen again. And the police weren't doing anything about it. For years and years.

You'd think something like that would scare you straight, but you become numb to it. We were on high alert, though. We were watching each other on the stroll, you know—'walking the streets'—and one night, one of my girlfriends was having a bad date. She was screaming, so I went over to see what was going down. The doors of the guy's truck were open, and she's got a knife pointed at the guy, and I said, 'Buddy, whatever is goin' down here, you need to pay up, count your losses, and get out of here.'

I crossed the street—I was on the way to see my dealer—and he gunned his engine and pulled out and hit me with his truck. Knocked me flying—ten feet, and I rolled over on my back, laid there for a few minutes, and then I got up, 'cause I was on a mission. I had to meet my dealer. I was hungry, and I needed 'food.' (We called drugs 'food' on the streets.)

I then went over to a hotel to call a friend—we were going to share my food—and after I made the call, some guy grabbed me and dragged me into this huge conference hall. There were two hundred people circled up, and he said, 'Hey, I think you need to be here.'

I'm sure he told me it was a Cocaine Anonymous meeting, but all I heard was 'cocaine,' and I'm like, *This is great. I'm going to find some more coke here.*

And then everybody started doing the Serenity Prayer, which I had no idea what it was back then. I had no idea what was going down. I was trying to figure out which one of the guys I could hook up with, when the guy who brought me into the meeting started to explain, 'This is Cocaine Anonymous. It means we don't do coke anymore.'

I was petrified. I'm like, *Everybody's going to know I'm high. I've got to get out of here.*

Looking back, there was a seed that was planted. There were seeds planted all over the place, kind of like a dot-to-dot picture. You connect enough of the dots, it starts to makes sense, and you can see the picture.

The next day, I couldn't feel my legs. I couldn't walk. I guess the shock of being hit by the truck had worn off, and I was in serious pain. But because I'd used the ambulances and hospitals so many times—faking injuries and trying to get free drugs off them—they said, 'No way. We know you.' It was the boy that cried wolf, but in a bad way.

It took two weeks before I could get any help. I finally had to phone my family, and they were able to convince the hospital that I was really hurt. Little did I know that before the truck hit me, I had endocarditis. It's a bacterial infection that starts in the heart. In my case it spread and caused an infection in my hip bone. It was so bad, the infection was spreading to my spine, so I always say, 'Thank God I was hit by a truck!' If I hadn't been hospitalized, they wouldn't have found the infection. It would have gone into my spine, and I would have been paralyzed. That was the second time I was told I was never going to walk again.

You'd think that with the insanity of all that, you'd stop, but you don't. It's so powerful. I would do whatever I needed to do to get my 'food.' By now, it wasn't about belonging; it wasn't about my girlfriends. It was anything *but* community. Now it was, *Try to hide and be invisible.* From everybody. And the best way to do that is to be the low of the lows. Just stay off the radar.

That's what I did. I shuffled myself from city to city. I knew which areas to go to. I knew how to find people who were into the things I was into—where to get drugs, and where to sell myself. You find that out real easy.

But as desperate as that was, there was that seed to keep going, keep fighting. I would go to treatment centers in Calgary, and Prince George, and I did a twenty-eight-day treatment in Vancouver. When I graduated from their program I decided to test myself, to see how my 'tool belt' was working—whether all the stuff I learned in rehab would actually get me anywhere. So I went down Hastings and Main, and for the next three years I had a $300-a-day heroin addiction. So that didn't work out all that well.

I brought myself back to Calgary, and friends were still going missing. I was either in jail, or hospital, or working the streets—the endless treadmill. You can stay on that treadmill as long as your legs will hold up, going nowhere. I'd sell myself for drugs, do the drugs, and then sell myself. It's insane, but you'd tell yourself, *I'm the one making this choice. I'm in control. I'm my own boss.* It's just such a façade. You're doing bad things, but you tell yourself they're not that bad. *At least you're not doing what 'they're' doing...*

But I was lying to myself. I remember giving women shit for taking dates for anything less than $40, and yet I'm taking dates for $20. It used to be if I didn't make decent money, I'd tell the john, 'f**k you,' and I'd get another guy, but I was so desperate I'd take a $20 date. If I got really lucky, and I marked somebody coming from the oil fields, they'd take me to a hotel for a day or two. But for all the money I was making, I couldn't hold on to it. As soon as it came to me, it was gone. Up my nose or in my arm.

It was bad. I was in Edmonton one *winter*, that's how out my mind I was, freezing, on crutches 'cause I couldn't use my legs, and my body was so diseased they wouldn't give me a hip operation until I got off the needle. As long as I was injecting, the hospital would have nothing to do with me.

But there were some good places, like George Beattie Detox. I would go with the intention of going into treatment—I probably went five times, and it was my 'home away from home.' I'd tell myself, *This is it, I'm going to do it*, but after a couple of days of eating and sleeping, you delude yourself and think, *I'm okay now. I'm healthy now. I'm good to go again*. Thing is, I never followed any of what I was told in the program. I'd take parts of it, but it was going to be *my* way.

I'd be out on the stroll, and the Salvation Army Crossroads van would come by. You get shot on the street for sharing anything, but in the Salvation Army van, it was my little break. They were so kind. I always had it in the back of my mind that if they had a place in their shelter to take me, I would go. But I would never ask for it. There's so much shame involved.

■ ■ ■

I had managed to get myself a little apartment. I remember sitting there thinking, *This is it. I've arrived!* I had a plan—I was going to get people together, and we'd be a family. We'd help each other out, look after each other. I was sitting there feeding this dream, getting high, thinking, *Okay, who are you going to invite in?*

Then the reality hit.

There wasn't anybody in my life who wasn't going to jack me, or stab me, or steal my drugs. Everything in my life felt like it was broken.

I thought, *Seriously—you've lived on the streets all these years; this is your dream, your hope—to have a family—and only now you realize how insane it is, that there's no one. There's no one.*

That sent me into self-abuse mode, and I shot up like crazy. Because I needed a hip replacement, I'd never shoot up in my legs. But I couldn't get a vein anywhere else. Everything was calloused or collapsed. I had nowhere to hit myself. Nowhere except my legs, and I knew that that meant abscesses. My whole system was pretty weak and sickly by then.

I shot up, and both my legs swelled to the size of watermelons. I was screaming with pain. I *had* to phone the ambulance. They took me to the hospital. Lying there, looking at my legs, I thought, *What is wrong with you? You still don't want to quit?* My whole body was sick; it was so tired, it was dying. Moments later, the doctor told me, 'I don't know how you made it this long. I don't think we're going to be able to save your legs. Your abscesses are so bad we may have to amputate.'

My first thought? *Oh God, I have to phone my dealer.*

Not, *I'm going to lose my legs*; no—*I've got to phone my dealer.* Until it happens, it's not real. Escape, escape, escape.

In the end, they didn't have to cut my legs off, and after I left the hospital I contacted the Bonnyville detox 'cause I had to disappear from the system. It was so backdoor—apparently, I work well that way—my plan was to go into treatment, and get the courts off my back.

At detox, the staff were always kind to me. They got me a bed in there, and I remember the fireworks going off on New Year's Eve night, so I *know* that was my clean date, December 31st. Kind of funny, isn't it? I'm going to get sober on the biggest party night of the year!

I went from there to Wellsprings, a one-year treatment program. It's faith-based, and this had me living around Christians 24-7. I'd been in treatment before, but this was different. This was God-centered. Not me-centered. *Huge* difference.

I'd had the sponsors. I'd done the Steps. I was going to meetings, doing everything everybody was telling me, but I just couldn't get it. Part of it was the obsession, the craving. The craving would always drag me back. You have seventy thousand thoughts a day; sixty-nine thousand would be about drugs and alcohol. That's all I knew; that's all my worth was. My whole identity.

At Wellsprings we were doing Bible studies and praying, and I would sit back, asking questions to fight against the idea that God was there—'Where was God when I was getting raped? Where was he when I got thrown out of a two-story window?'—and then I thought, *Look, you're going to be here a year. Why don't you try asking questions that show you that he is here? What's the worst that could happen? You'd get clean. That wouldn't be so bad.*

That's what I did. I went outside and said, 'Okay God, if you're here, then you need to take my craving away. You need to show me. If you're this all-powerful God, then you need to show me.'

I waited a few minutes, and nothing happened. I didn't feel anything. I thought I ought to feel something...

Two weeks later, I was doing my chores, and I thought, *Hey, when's the last time I thought of drugs? When's the last time I thought about getting high?* I tried to pinpoint it, so I could share this secret and *everybody* could get saved. But I couldn't. I couldn't pinpoint it, but I knew I had done it. I knew it had happened.

In my mind I'm thinking, *Look at you! You did this! You conquered it!* Then I heard this voice, not in my mind, but in my heart, 'Oh no you didn't! This is ME!' That was my first WOW. That was my first answered *prayer* prayer. Not a begging, hopeless prayer, but a real asking prayer. Wow. That was BIG. Until then, I was fighting. Until then I couldn't let go.

The next thing was I had to show up in court. The prosecutor was asking for seven-year pen time. I couldn't do seven years in prison. I had put a little slip of paper in my bra. I'd written on it Isaiah 12:2: 'Surely God is my salvation; I will trust and not be afraid. The LORD, the LORD himself, is my strength and my defense; he has become my salvation.' And I prayed hard. I didn't want to go to jail; that was the most terrifying thing I could think of—locked in a jail cell with your own thoughts. I now know you don't have to be locked in a jail cell to do that—you can be imprisoned by your own thoughts wherever you are.

I went to court with some of the staff from Wellsprings, and they told the judge how good I was doing. He sentenced me to a deuce less a day, which was *unheard* of. Two years less a day meant I wasn't going to do time. This was a huge turning point for me. At the Bible studies at Wellsprings, people were talking about their own personal relationship with God, and I was thinking, *Well, how does that work?* I didn't exactly have much success with relationships. People said that God gave them signs, and I didn't know what they were talking about. I went out for a walk and a smoke, and after about a hundred yards, the smoke went out. I lit it again, walked some more, and it went out again. I thought, *Is this the sign that they're all talking about? Nah, God doesn't work like that.* I lit up, walked on, and the smoke went out, again. I stopped and I looked up, and there was a billboard that said, 'And you still don't get it?'

I thought, *I'm on a roll here!* So I decided to try and quit smoking. I said, 'God, I don't want to have this next smoke.' I didn't say, 'I want to quit smoking'; I said, 'God, I don't want to have this *next* smoke,' just like they do at Alcoholics Anonymous. I didn't have that smoke. Or the next one I wanted. Or the next one. That's how I quit smoking.

Since that time, I've seen signs *everywhere*. God took the old lenses off, and put new ones on, and now I'm able to see signs everywhere—through TV, through people, through birds flying in the sky—my spirit inside has come alive. The little girl inside me that was sleeping—she has woken up.

■ ■ ■

Part of the Wellspring's program was community service. One of the women I used to meet on their outreaches asked if I wanted to ride along with them in their van. I was only three months clean, and I was worried that I'd jump *out* of the van and start partying with some of the people I knew, so I said no, but I asked if I could come later.

A few weeks later I felt maybe I should try, and it was great! Out on the streets, all I ever did was take. Now I was starting to give back. I started sitting on community boards with people who mentored me and who are now my new friends. They all walk beside me. Sometimes it feels so bizarre, like *How did you get from that street corner to here?*

I started going to Salvation Army Church on 117th, and this summer I was looking out the window, and seriously, it was twenty feet from where I used to work, and I thought,

How is it that it took me thirty-five years to get from that corner and into the church?

Ever since I've been on this walk with God, he's put people and opportunities in my path and opened doors for me. I keep going through everything he opens up to me. Sometimes I don't *know* that it's him, but I look back, and, yeah, I know. It's him.

One of the doors God opened to me was Women's Journey. Two of my new friends from the Salvation Army told me about this pamper weekend, and it sounded wonderful. At the time, I was living in a house full of women—like thirty to thirty-five women. Any kind of break from that would be a gift! My friend Sonja and I got invited to one of these weekends, and we got driven way out of town—which freaked us out, given we had no idea where we were going. We arrived at this huge house, and they gave us a tour. It had three dining rooms—with gold and silver cutlery. I remember thinking, *Why doesn't anybody steal this?* The more we looked around, the more valuables we saw. I remember thinking, *Jackpot!* But then I thought, *They're letting us come here to stay. That doesn't make sense. Why would they do that—the likes of us in a place like this?*

We had group sessions, and we got to swim in their pool, and come nighttime as soon as I laid down, *I went to sleep.* That had not happened in twenty-some years. For twenty years, I was paranoid that people were going to come to get me while I'm sleeping. That night, for the first time, I felt safe.

The next day was this full-on pampering thing. I didn't feel it the first day, but by the second day, I felt this presence in the house. All the people running it were volunteering.

They weren't getting paid to do it, and that just blew me away. Everybody was being so friggin' *nice*. People were doing kind things and not getting nothing in return.

Up until then, I believed that nobody cares. Nobody cared about *me*. Nobody's going to know if you're dying, if you're going to be that next 'Missing' poster. And then these people come into my life, and they're loving me, valuing me—no matter what. By Sunday I felt, *Yeah, this is real. There's no ulterior motive. They don't want nothing from me. What I have to offer is a broken me, and they're okay with that.*

I had never had this feeling in my life.

When the weekend was over, I wanted more. I said, 'When can we come back?' They told me that they run the weekends four times a year and asked if I'd like to volunteer for the next one. That was six years ago, and every three months I've volunteered at Women's Journey, ever since.

■　■　■

Because of what I went through, I had to put the little girl inside me to sleep. The little girl that was *me*. The wild, adventurous, curious, ready-for-anything little girl—she had to go to sleep 'cause there was too much pain. So much had died. So much was destructive. So much was hopeless. Jesus talks about being reborn, and I think that's what happened to my little girl. She woke up.

Now, instead of the destruction, there's construction. Not only for my life, but for those around me. I used to be despairing; now I'm full of hope. The breakthrough came because I found God. He found me. We found each other! I finally introduced myself, and he showed me who he was.

Way back, when I gave the world the finger and an 'Up yours!' it was the start of my downhill journey. That turned around with my surrender, when I asked God to show me that he was there with me. God has given me a life that's an unopened gift, and there's something new, every single day.

STICKERS ONLY STICK
WHEN YOU LET THEM

Not forgiving is like drinking rat poison and
then waiting for the rat to die.[1]

ANNE LAMOTT

To be healed of shame we do not deserve, we must, sooner
or later, come to terms with our feelings about the person
or persons who shamed us. ... We cannot undo what was
done to us. We have been wounded, and we carry our
woundedness as part of our unchangeable reality. The
only reality we can alter is the reality of our feelings. ...

The hard remedy of forgiveness is the only remedy
we have. ... Revenge does not heal; it only makes
things worse. Forgetting does not help ... it just
festers as the poisonous source of other pains.[2]

LEWIS B. SMEDES

There is no future without forgiveness.[3]

DESMOND TUTU

Heidi's mother, Charlotte, was a gospel singer. She toured throughout the US and Canada as a member of The Happy Ferrens, and later as a soloist scheduled to open for the Blackwood Brothers and the Oak Ridge Boys. All that changed when she was raped by a man she thought was a friend. One night, as she was confiding in him, he turned on her. One moment she was sharing her faith and talking about the man she wanted to marry, and the next moment a jealous, violent rage was unleashed. As she was being violated, the rapist compounded his abuse by telling her, "You'll never sing again."

Charlotte didn't know what to do. She didn't report the rape, and no one knew about it—until her pregnancy made it obvious. A sad fact of life is that sometimes it's the people who love you the most who can do the most damage. Her family and friends told her she was "ruined," and advised her to marry her rapist—after all, no one else would have her now.

She didn't, but he stayed in her life—and continued the violence. At one point he shoved a shopping cart into her stomach in an attempt to abort the baby.

Everyone wanted Charlotte to get an abortion. Even her ministers told her to abort. She wouldn't do it. Charlotte gave birth to Heidi, but they couldn't get away from the man who was her father because her family tried to make him a part of their lives. It wasn't unconditional inclusion, however. None of them would ever leave *their* kids alone with him. He was good enough for Charlotte, but not good enough for them.

He was so physically abusive towards Heidi that he broke one of her legs. And by the time she was four years old, he thought that she needed to "experience things." That's when the molestation began. Heidi's mother tried several times to take Heidi and get away from him. Like a man obsessed, he kept tracking them down. Heidi was in the crosshairs. On several occasions, he attempted to kidnap Heidi. He also tried to take custody of her by placing an ad in a different city, saying she had been stolen by her mother. It became clear that Charlotte had to fight back, so she filed restraining orders, which he breached. Then she filed criminal charges against him for the rape.

In the interim, Heidi was placed in foster care because her father distorted the facts and told the social workers that, with all the moves, her mother was a flight risk. He also manipulated the truth and said that Charlotte was unable to care for Heidi due to her disabilities. Years earlier, Charlotte had fallen down an elevator shaft and nearly died. While she made what many believed to be a miraculous recovery, she was nonetheless seriously disabled and had to endure rigorous physical therapy.

In foster care, Heidi's nightmare continued. She cried the whole time. She couldn't eat and lived in constant fear. The foster parents beat her and said that if she wouldn't eat, they wouldn't feed her, so she starved. They also molested her. When the parents weren't abusing her, their teenage sons took turns.

The foster parents also threatened Heidi—telling her that if she didn't visit her father, she would never see her mother again. She was terrified. Her social worker intervened and told Heidi that she didn't have to see her father if she didn't want to. He was the first person to tell her that she had a choice.

Things eventually led to a custody trial. It was revealed that Charlotte was not the only one; her father had also assaulted seven women. Even though Heidi was a child, she testified about his molestation. He pled insanity and was released to seek psychiatric help. Heidi and her mother were reunited and moved states to get away from him. Charlotte worked several jobs to try to support them—teaching music lessons, part-time office jobs, and retail. Because of her disabilities, it made for a hard life for her and Heidi.

■ ■ ■

HOMELESSNESS HAPPENS. NOBODY EVER PLANS to be homeless. It's gradual. By the time I was twenty-one, our money just ran out. My mother's health had degenerated, and she was very, very sick. I was working two jobs, and you'd think that working that hard you could have something come from it. It didn't. For over a year, we were sleeping in our car, and I would sneak food out to my mom from the hotel cafeteria where I worked. It got to the place where it felt like there was no way out.

It didn't matter how hard I worked or how much money I earned, I never had enough for a deposit on an apartment. I was still paying bills on our house back in Arkansas. It hadn't sold, so I was still paying for a house that we couldn't afford. It was this cycle that just kept us right where we were. But we needed money. We were nearly starving. Something had to change. I'll never forget the night I stood outside a strip club. I stared at the neon sign, and I thought, *Could I do that? I could do that. I could dance.* I was desperate. What else could I do? As I watched the men coming and going, the thought was terrifying. I knew enough to know that life in the strip club is glamorized. They make it look like you're going to make so much money, but it's a lie.

I believe God intervened that night because just when I had almost mustered the courage to see if I could dance, I saw a black van parked beside the strip club. I could see the man sitting in it. And in that moment I knew I couldn't do it. If I went in and danced, I was making everything that had happened to me okay. I knew if I started stripping, I would constantly be seeing flashes of my father in every man in front of me, and that I would be telling them that it was okay for them to look at me in that way and treat me like that was all I was worth.

If I did that, I knew I just couldn't live with myself. I said, *I'm not gonna go there. I may have nothing, and I may be homeless, but I am not going to let that happen in my life. There's got to be something more.*

Then my mom got really sick. Her feet turned black. I took her to hospital, but after a few days of treatment they figured that, as she was homeless, she couldn't pay, so they turned her out of the hospital. I made the decision then that we were going to drive back to Arkansas. At least we could live in our house for a while.

When we got back, the house was in really bad shape. While we were gone, a racoon had moved in, and he had destroyed the place. And we'd given everything away before we left for California because that's what my mom is like. She'd just give stuff to someone that needed it rather than try to make $2 trying to sell it. Now *we* were the ones that had absolutely nothing. I called our church in Arkansas, and that was hard. Before we'd left for the West Coast, they'd thrown a big party for us, and everybody had said, 'Heidi's going away to do great things,' and I believed it.

It was very humbling to make that phone call and say, 'Things did not work out the way I thought they were going to. Mom is sick.' The church family was amazing. They welcomed us back with open arms. I couldn't have asked for a better church family. They brought us some furniture and a mattress—and they helped us evict the raccoon and clean up his mess!

They also brought us bags of clothes. I had always wanted a black turtleneck. It was one of those small things that you never tell anyone 'cause it's silly. But God knows. And in a bag of clothes one of the church women had given me, I pulled out a black turtleneck, and it was kind of like, everything's going to be okay.

❖ ❖ ❖

But living happily ever after only happens in fairy tales. Because I knew how much my mom had gone through, I grew up wanting to be a source of love and care for her. It always made me really happy when she was happy. I became a people-pleaser. I also grew up with a longing for a father-figure who would truly love me. Those two things got me into a lot of trouble because I trusted older men in my life far too quickly, and many of them behaved inappropriately with me—including some of my pastors.

I kept getting preyed upon by men of a certain age, and it wasn't any better in my dating relationships. They were abusive. By the time I went to college, I had become really angry because I felt like I was stuck in this fated destiny. I was angry because I felt like I had no other choice for my life. I had all of these strikes against me—born a child of rape, raised without a father, molested, abused, poor, homeless. I was so scared of being a victim, but I felt I had no way to prevent becoming one over and over again. I hate the word 'victim' because a victim has had all her power taken away. I was so mad I decided that I wasn't going to let that happen.

I thought long and hard about my life, and I remembered the times when I felt I had the most strength and joy. It was when I was helping other people. What stood out the most was the volunteer work I did at the local Rape Crisis Center. Since I was a kid, I'd really enjoyed the performing arts. At the Crisis Center, I did this event where we improvised different scenarios for young trainees, new helpline workers, and the organization's volunteers. In the scene that I performed, I played a woman who had been raped. I was trying to tell my boyfriend what had happened, but my boyfriend didn't believe me. There was a whole lot of my life in that improvisation, and I wasn't sure if I did a very good job acting it out.

Later that day, one of the founders of the organization came up to me, and she was in tears. She said, 'The woman you portrayed—that was my story. When I was raped, I tried to tell my boyfriend, and he didn't believe me. He told me it was my fault and made me feel like I was to blame. I've carried it around with such shame my whole life. I've been helping to run this organization for years, and I have never told anyone that story before now. That scene you did today—it's the first time I knew it *wasn't* my fault.'

I realized then that every single thing I had gone through enabled me to do something with it that could bless somebody else. And I just couldn't think of a better thing to do with my life. I knew that I wanted to help people through storytelling for the rest of my life. Stories allowed me to escape as a little girl. I even recited my favorite story on the witness stand at my father's trial—I had to prove that a four-year-old was capable of remembering more details than the defense thought I could. Stories saved my life, and now I was determined to give others the same refuge I had found.

I was very fortunate to be accepted into the Deleware Professional Theater Training Program. Not only was it free; they *paid* me to go! While I was studying there, I had the opportunity to be a voice and movement coach for a special program.

An actor has to create the character they're portraying. You have to develop their backstory. You have to get into who this person is, and how they got to be that way. And to do that really well, you have to be able to step outside of yourself, so you can see life and feel it in new ways—because you're no longer you; you're the character you're portraying. You're creating a living, breathing person, and she speaks in a certain way, and she moves in a certain way, and she has a certain kind of life. All of those aspects communicate things about who that character is. If you do it well, that character is different than who you are in and of yourself.

All of that is a near miraculous opportunity. Being able to isolate those specific aspects of character enables a person to realize, *Oh! If the character I'm portraying has good posture, and I can pull that off on-stage, then off-stage—I don't have to slouch! And I don't have to speak in a particular way.* I spent many of my growing-up years in rural Arkansas—and I can put on a Southern drawl with the best of them—if I choose to. But it goes even deeper than that: it's like changing scripts.

From my personal background, I have a script that creates a character that has a guilt complex. It's a script that says: 'We knew she was gonna mess up out there—a child of rape ... her lack of a father-figure ... the sexual abuse. ... That's why she has such bad taste in men.'

When we let other people write the script for our stories, and we become the people *they* think we should be, we give away our power. But that's not at all who *I* want to be. Who *do* I want to be? What script do I want to read from? We can all make those kinds of choices. Choices that are completely separate from our history and our circumstances.

If you're able to separate what you think you know about yourself, or separate what the world says you should be, then you can say, 'Well, I can't change my story. I can't change what happened to me. I *can* change the way it shows up on my person and the way I carry myself—the way I choose to react to life. I can create the kind of life I want to live by choosing how I show up in the world. I can put the pieces together and make that life, even if initially it feels weird and fake. One day I will be that person.'

That thing, or kind of person, that's sitting somewhere outside of myself that I tell myself I can never be—I am that now, and it's been amazing.

This 'rescripting' has been a gift I got from my mother. She used to read me a children's story by Max Lucado.[4] It's about these little wooden people called Wemmicks. In Wemmickville, where they live, they sing a song: 'The getting and giving of stickers is what we do day after day.' Every day, the Wemmicks stick gold stars on the pretty people—those with smooth wood and nice paint—as well as on the ones who are talented and perform well. They always get stars: 'Stars are for stars.' Then there are the unfortunate ones. Those who don't seem to do anything important or who are always messing up; those who are clumsy or are damaged in some way—they get ugly gray dots stuck on them. And the thing about the stickers—they never come off.

But there's one little wooden Wemmick who's different. Nothing sticks to her—no stars, no dots. That's because she knows that the stickers only stick if you let them. She won't let them stick, because she knows the wood carver, the Maker, the One who made her, the One who knows her by name. She knows that the Maker loves her very much. So it doesn't matter to her what the other Wemmicks think about her.

The whole performance piece that so many of us live by has us desperately trying to earn stars, and do our best to give the dots a miss. But each of us can realize, *I don't want to live that way.* That's how I understand the power of forgiveness. In my teens and early twenties, I was filled with an anger that was hurting me. I was allowing the pain from my past to compound and hurt me in more permanent ways than I could see—even though I'd be holding on to a toilet, throwing up everywhere because I had ulcers. I learned that forgiveness is as much about your own well-being as it is anything else.

I wanted those who had hurt me so deeply to be held accountable. I wanted them to be given a great big gray dot for what they did to me. And I wanted to hear them say, 'I'm sorry.' But if that's what matters most to you, you lose out on what's possible for yourself. Because if you can't let that go, that resentment, it creates sickness. The more you are looking for them to make it okay, the more power you give away, and the more you lose your freedom. You lose your ability to be a source of light in your own life and the lives of others.

This is what I've had to do with my father. I desperately wanted him to pay the price for all he did to my mother and me. But he hasn't. When he pled insanity, he wasn't sent to prison; he wasn't even registered as a sex offender. He was supposed to admit himself into psychiatric care, but he only went to a counselor for a couple of weeks. He was very handsome, and very charming, and he basically talked himself out of the need for therapy. It's the, 'If the man is handsome, he couldn't possibly have raped her. He couldn't be a bad guy. He looks so presentable. She must have wanted it in some way.' So much of our world allows beauty to do the storytelling, and we get seduced by something we think is attractive and okay.

When most people are victimized, they become the victim. The label sticks. The victimization defines them. It determines the character they play in life. When you go through a lot, or you've been put through a lot because of the things that have happened to you, there is a kind of dark and silent blame that stays inside of you. I used to be tormented by thoughts like, *If only I had been in another room. If only I had been a better child. If only I had done this or if I had done that.*

But 'victim' is only a sticker that sticks if you let it. Just because you were victimized, just because you had this thing happen, it does not mean that's you or that's your life. I am a person. Things happened. Horrible things. I wanted my father to recognize what he had done, and I wanted an apology. There came a point where I realized that would never happen.

My father was diagnosed as a paranoid schizophrenic and a sociopath. The courts, and even my extended family, tried to use his history as a way to justify what he did, that he himself was a victim. In fact, my father once told me that he was just as much a victim as I was. And it just hit me—there's no excuse for what he did. None. He had a choice. *I* have a choice. I would never get what I wanted from him, and when it came down to it, I cared more about my future than holding him accountable for my past.

I *can* keep my focus on all the trauma I've suffered. I can choose to dwell in the trauma, and keep reliving it. But if I do that, bitterness rises up and takes over because my father hasn't paid for all that he's done to my mother and me. I know enough to know that bitterness is like poison. It poisons my life, and when it's at work in me, it poisons those around me. My bitterness affects them. If you dwell in the traumatized past, then there's no redemptive future; there's nowhere to go but for your past life to keep repeating itself, whether you like it or not. We each have a future, and my trauma doesn't own me. I own *it*.

■　■　■

Forgiving myself has been a really hard thing to do, but I know that forgiveness has to start with me. I heard a preacher say that the word 'forgive' in the Lord's Prayer—'forgive us our sins, as we have forgiven those who sin against us'5—it means to 'let go.' 'Let go of our sins, as we have let go of those who've sinned against us.' It made me think of the work I've done as an acting coach. I've worked with some people who posture themselves protectively. They look down at the ground; they don't make eye contact; their shoulders are slumped and rounded. Physiologically, they're protecting themselves—and—they're spending all their energy holding on to what traumatized them. Physiologically, they're holding *in* what traumatized them. Their whole body posture is an attempt to protect what feels so very vulnerable. If I can get them to lift their heads and look up; if they'll pull their shoulders back and stand up straight; if they'll take a deep breath and let it fully out—if they'll take all that they're carrying, and let it go—it's monumental!

I tend to analyze everything, even in my prayer time. But as I've spent a long time praying about all of this, I've recognized how silly it is to be holding on to the pain and the anger, and I've realized that there are things I don't have control over; things I won't *ever* have control over—but in those moments, I can choose to let go of the damage that was done and bless those who have sinned against me. Letting go is the power of forgiveness. And it's a choice. I either choose to hold on to the hurt, hold on to the trauma, hold on to the anger and the rage—and I've certainly had times where I held all of that in close—or I can let it all go. Especially as I speak blessing over it all, there comes some sort of distancing from it, and a peace washes over it all. A tangible peace that is as tangible as the terror. When I'm able to do that, then I get to be the hero of my own story.

I want to take my past, everything in it, all that happened to me, and use it to help others in their pain. I am so grateful because I am who I am, and I am who I am because of all that I have overcome. I have the ability to connect with people and help people in a deeper way than I ever could have if I had had what some people consider a 'perfect life' ... a beautiful, pain-free life.

My family has served in every conflict since the American Revolution, and growing up, my mom used to take me to veterans hospitals to sing with her. I loved doing that—trying to support our service members any way I could. When I finished my rigorous classical theater training program in graduate school, I was 'supposed' to become a 'serious' actor. You don't *just* sing and dance. But one of my childhood friends had been wounded on tour in Iraq, outside of Fallujah. He was always one of those people that lights up every room. And now he had third-degree burns over three-quarters of his body. I thought if there was anyone that was going to take something so horrible and use it to make the world a better place, it would be him. He inspired me.

I'm the last and longest running 'Miss USO.'[6] For six years I've toured throughout Europe, the Middle East, and Asia as an ambassador, performer, spokesperson, and steward of gratitude for service members and their families. I've been blessed to perform and speak in some incredible venues—Madison Square Garden, Times Square at New Year's Eve, in television programs and films, and in front of four US Presidents, two Prime Ministers, the Queen of Uganda and hundreds of international dignitaries—but the performances and moments that have always touched me the most were in small towns and military hospitals, spending one-on-one time with our heroes.

As a foster child, the loss of home was very traumatic for me. When you are four years old, and suddenly everything you know, everything you think makes you safe in this world is ripped away from you, it is utterly terrifying. It isn't dissimilar to what our men and women in uniform experience both on and off the battlefield. They're far from home, and nothing is safe. I always found music and kindness provide a refuge.

It meant so much to me as a little girl to have someone sing a song I loved when I was lonely, or care enough to stay with me when I was scared. Those things matter. Our idea of home, what we identify as 'home' is extremely important.

Human beings are miraculous. When we are called to things greater than ourselves, it makes what some consider ordinary, extraordinary. Our men and women in uniform are the definition of that, and they daily do extraordinary things as though they were ordinary. It is one of the greatest joys of my life to support them, to encourage them, and be some sort of connection to what they've left back home.

I'll never forget one of my first performances with the USO during New York City's Fleet Week. The Coast Guard were shuttling us to the venue in vans, and the bulk of our team were laughing at the front of the vehicle, having a grand time. I saw a large, tough-looking and thoughtful man sitting alone in the back of the van, so I went to say hello. He said, 'USO, huh? They performed while I was in Vietnam. Bob Hope, Raquel Welch, it was great—but you know what the best part was? After the show was over, Raquel Welch came over to the tents and hung out with us for hours. It was the first time I had a sense of home again.' He started to tear up. 'That saved me, that day. I hadn't been home in ages and having her care enough not just to perform—which was great, don't get me wrong—but that she made me feel human, it made me remember my home, the people I love, and why I was there in the jungle. It saved me.'

After hearing his story, I swore I would always do that. I knew just how important it was to have light in the darkness, and I knew that I could and would always strive to bring people the light.

BABY STEPS

When the fear of staying the same is greater than
the fear of change, then you will change. ...

Basically the brokenness that has gone on in [the lives of
exploited women] has somehow to be healed. ... You only know
you are a human being who is lovable when people actually
love you, when you actually recognize that somebody does
care. I think that when women realize that they are lovable
and deserve to be respected, no matter what they have done
or where they have been, then there is a transformation.[1]

JODY RAPHAEL

Terrika has worked as a probation officer in Los Angeles for the past thirteen years. For the past eight years, she has worked in a specialized unit servicing commercially sexually exploited children. She conducts assessments of all the youth that are picked up by police detectives and patrol officers in Los Angeles County and assigns them to a probation officer. She also facilitates weekly meetings with the public defender, the district attorney advocacy agencies, the Department of Child and Family Services, the Department of Mental Health, and the Department of Public Health. Together they discuss the services that should surround each youth, and attend to their immediate needs. This multi-agency partnership responds case by case, to facilitate the long-term safety and stability of the youth. Terrika is also involved with a specialized court that works specifically with trafficked youth, in direct consultation with the probation officers.

The following are her reflections on her work with at-risk girls.

■ ■ ■

GROWING UP, I WANTED TO be a therapist, and I am currently working on a Master's in Marital and Family Therapy. After I graduated with my first degree, I became a case manager with the YWCA of Greater Los Angeles, working with at-risk youth. A year later, a job opportunity came up for detention officers to work in a juvenile hall in south-central LA. I love working with kids, and I felt like I could make a difference. I got the job, but it wasn't what I expected.

I thought I'd be helping kids, and they'd receive me with open arms. But it was much harder than I thought.

I'm from a smaller town in California, Bakersfield, so life in LA was an adjustment, to say the least—especially the inner city. In juvenile hall I worked in the girls unit, and that's when I first became involved with 'prostituted girls.' Back then, that's what I called it—*prostitution*—because that was all I knew. It wasn't until later, eight years ago when I started getting training, I realized that they weren't teenage prostitutes—they were commercially sexually exploited children. There's a huge difference between seeing and treating a girl as a prostitute and as one who's been sexually exploited. I've never met a girl who told herself, *When I grow up, I want to be a prostitute.* There's always coercion. Somebody's groomed her. And usually, there's someone threatening her if she doesn't make her quota.

■ ■ ■

In June 2011, LA County had been identified as a major hub for sexual exploitation, and a supervisor approached me and told me she was starting a program targeting commercially sexually exploited youth. She wanted a female probation officer to work with the girls. After extensive training we started the CSEC program in January 2012. CSEC stands for Commercially Sexually Exploited Children, and I've been with the program from the ground up. We work with girls between the ages of eleven and eighteen, and by the time we see them, many of the girls have already been in 'the life'—exploited—two or three years. Many of them have been criminalized for behavior they've been forced into by their exploiters.

The majority of the girls I've worked with have come from foster care. And the majority of them have been sexually abused. Many of the girls that have not been in foster care also have an underlying history of past sexual abuse. That's the common denominator. But simply put, those exploited can be anyone's daughter. Anyone's daughter can be manipulated by a male that's up to no good.

A girl I'll call 'Marie' was the first commercially sexually exploited youth I supervised on my caseload with CSEC. I was nervous, and eager to help, but even after all the training I had received, I knew there was still so much to learn from 'real life' experiences. Marie was sixteen years old and had been placed in a group home. She had been trafficked since the age of eleven. Prior to her exploitation, she had endured sexual abuse, and because of her poor behavior, her adoptive mother wanted to relinquish her parental rights. She wanted nothing more to do with Marie.

The bad behavior continued at the group home. Marie was very assaultive towards her peers and was verbally abusive towards staff. She often trashed the group home. I was constantly going to meetings about her behavior. She would sincerely apologize for acting out and would do well for a short period of time, but it wasn't long before she'd have another meltdown. It got so bad that I told her if she kept the negative behavior up, I would have to send her to a locked facility. The threat didn't change her behavior—and at the time, I didn't realize that being locked up was part of her childhood trauma. The day I was going to lock her up, she ran away. Though I was disappointed in her behavior and wanted her accountable for her actions, I learned a lot that day. I learned that punishment is not the answer.

As weeks and months went by, Marie maintained contact with me via telephone to let me know she was alright. On one particular occasion she called me, crying hysterically. She said she was tired. She also told me she was using (drugs). I bit my tongue because I knew it was not the time to scold her. It was not the time to tell her that she was wrong for leaving the placement. My sole job in the moment was to listen and be of support. I allowed her to guide the direction of those phone calls, and I let her know I was glad that she was safe. Eventually, I was able to encourage her to return to the group home. She slowly settled in, graduated high school, and went on to college.

Marie is now a survivor advocate who returns to the juvenile halls to speak to other youth who have been trafficked and struggle to get away from their traffickers. She speaks in front of hundreds of people, teaching them about the effects of trafficking and how she overcame it. She's a living example of redemption. Her strength and resilience continue to inspire me.

Marie taught me the importance of building caring relationships. Had I not developed rapport early in the relationship, she may not have reached out for help, support, and guidance. She taught me that victims of trafficking need to feel love and support, not judgment. She also taught me patience. Any kind of change is hard, and only an overcomer works her way through trauma.

■ ■ ■

The first part in a girl's restoration is building relationships with caring adults. In my experience over the last eight years, this has been the most significant factor in enabling the girls to overcome their past and the trauma they've endured. But many of their Romeo pimps started out like loving adults, so it raises the big question, who do they trust? And why should they trust me?

That's the hard part. We're going up against a monster, one who has presented himself as a savior of some sort. Every day, we're fighting against the girl's Romeo boyfriend. He's been there when she's called, no matter what time, and no matter what trouble she's gotten herself into. And he's told her that no one else is there for her but him. When she calls her pimp, he's going to pick her up, no matter what their past relationship has been.

If I'm going to compete with that, I also have to be there when she calls. I have to be willing to build that relationship and demonstrate an even greater commitment to her. It won't happen overnight, but it will happen as long as I'm there when she calls. And it does happen—I was asked to be the god-mother of the baby of one of my old probationers. She's now in her late twenties. Several years earlier, while she was on the run, I tried my best to be there for her. No matter what she got herself into, I continued to show her my support. I wasn't ever punitive or heavy-handed. I knew that in order for me to help save her own life, I had to be there as a support. I had to con-tinue to build our relationship. So when she called, I answered. When all the girls I've worked with have called, I answered.

But I can't be on-call 24-7. It's so important to connect the girls to other people. They need a community of people that surround them. I call it the youth's personal 'wraparound team.' If I'm not available, another caring adult will act as her advocate. That's why CSEC is a multi-disciplinary partnership, so that we can extend the 24-7 care that the girls need.

One of the things that is clear to me is that for most of these girls, there weren't parents or caring, supportive, and appropriate adults in the picture. That's certainly true for the youth in foster care. For one reason or another, the girls didn't have somebody they trusted. When they needed help, when it came time to say, 'I got myself into trouble. I did something I didn't want to do, and I don't know what to do now,' there was no one there for them. Or they were afraid of being punished, so they kept their secrets to themselves.

I'm a single parent of two girls, and I know that sometimes I can overreact in some situations. I believe it's important that as parents we assess our own strengths and weaknesses when communicating with our children. It is vital for their protection and to prevent potential exploitation. That's one of the reasons I've intentionally connected my kids with people that they can talk to. I don't ever want my children to feel like they can't talk to me about something. But if they don't feel able to talk to me, they know that they can talk to their pediatrician, for example. Her clinic is just down the street from their school. They know her and they trust her.

■ ■ ■

Through my work with the child trafficking unit, I've learned that the thirteen- and fourteen-year-old girls can be the hardest to work with, due to the trauma-bonding with the trafficker. This is also true for newly-trafficked youth. Because of the trauma they've endured, and because of the bonding that they've had with their trafficker, it's very difficult for them to detach from that relationship. In their minds, he's been the most caring person in their lives. He's been the one who's been

most committed to them. He may well have been the most stable relationship they've ever had. It's not until they're sixteen,
seventeen, eighteen, and going into the transitional ages that
they start to be able to separate from the intensity of the relationship with their trafficker. Until then, they may not be ready
to open up or even process what they've been through. No
matter what, it is important that caring adults and advocates
are committed to their journey of healing and restoration.

Mistakes are a part of all of our lives. We all make them.
Remembering that helps me combat compassion fatigue.
When we've worked with a fifteen-year-old and helped to get
her stable, she's been in a group home for six months, and then
she relapses, it's very discouraging. We need to understand
that relapse is a part of the journey. It is for all of us! It's a part
of the Stages of Change.[2] I didn't understand that in the beginning. In my early years, whenever a girl would call me and say
that she was in trouble and needed help, I wanted to help and
see a complete change right away. I had big, grand plans for
her life, for a whole new future. Too often, I overwhelmed the
girls with all these goals and expectations. Now I try to help
them to plant their feet and stay in the here-and-now. I ask really simple questions: 'What can we do to go forward? We can't
change what has transpired, so where are we at, right now, and
what can I do to help you get to the next step?'

We take baby steps to help them stabilize. Let's say I have a
kid that is running away all the time. That's especially the case
with a lot of our foster youth. They're running away. In our
first interview, we simply ask them what they need. When they
feel like their voice is being heard, and that not all adults are
trying to run their lives for them, it settles them down. It's the
first step in bringing some stability to their lives.

That question, 'What do you need?' is the first step in the relationship-building process. If a girl has trouble expressing herself, if she won't talk to me, I ask, 'What are some baby steps you could take to meet your needs?' We try to break things down for her. We're not trying to solve her problem—we're just trying to help her to start moving in the right direction. What are some baby steps that could begin to stabilize her life in the next thirty days? That's the goal. It's the beginning of the larger goal of harm reduction. I am trying to prevent her from running away, and running back into situations that put her at risk.

Sometimes the group homes can be a barrier. If she arrives at a new group home with all of her personal belongings in a plastic garbage bag, and she's told that she's not going to get any clothes until she's been there for thirty days, that may trigger her to run. Why would she stay in a place that doesn't care for her? Her pimp bought her clothes. As the caring adult, or the probation officer, or the social worker, we need to help her with her basic needs. We need to help her with a clothing allowance. Those are the baby steps that start to stabilize her life. It sends her the message that we're there for her, that we understand her needs, and that we want to help.

As a caregiver, there's a tricky piece that seems to be counterintuitive, especially for the girls who've been in and out of the foster care system. When working with them, we want to address the trauma they've endured, and we want to address it right away. Every group home has a program, and the girls have to meet with a therapist, whether they like it or not. But these girls have been from therapist to therapist. They're 'therapied out.' So if a kid says she does not feel like going to the therapist, that's okay. It's okay for a kid to say, 'I don't want to talk about that right now.'

To make a child talk to somebody that they're not comfortable with is not helpful. Especially if it's a male. We all have people we don't want to talk to. It's unfair to make a girl talk to a male if she doesn't want to talk to him. So when you're talking about trauma, you have to understand what their triggers are. You have to really get to know a child and look at them as an individual. A cookie-cutter way of doing things in the foster system may not work with that child. You really need a holistic, individual approach, and that's really, really important.

That poses its own challenge. I've never asked a girl about her story … initially. It's natural to want to know her story, not because I'm trying to be nosy, but because I want to care. I want to understand her unique situation. But it's important that I don't ask those questions. Her story may be the only thing she feels she has control over, and her trust is only going to be earned by providing her with my support. We have to take advantage of 'moments.' That's all we have. We only have a moment. We don't know what a girl is facing. It may be suicidal thoughts. She may be facing incredible pressures— they're being recruited all the time by other girls—even in the group homes. They're being recruited when they go to school. She may have people who have threatened her life. These are all the things that she's carrying. Because of all of these pressures, she may be planning to run away tonight. You never know what can be a trigger.

Just a few weeks ago, I was having a rough day because we had a girl that had run away from her group home. She had been gone for about a month but had maintained contact with us. One day she texted her caseworker: 'I'm ready. I'm tired. I'm tired of doing this.' Within an hour, the police found her and picked her up. Due to her runaway status, officers had the discretion to detain. The caseworker asked me, 'Should I detain her?' She wasn't wanting to punish the girl. Rather, the caseworker was fearful of what might happen if she was released. We don't want this young teenager to die on the streets. We want to protect her. And sometimes we utilize detention because we feel it's the best way to protect her. Sometimes it seems like the *only* solution to very big problems.

It was a really hard decision because we often form tight-knit relationships with our girls. And we were scared for this girl. Detention was and has always been the protocol. Instead, we re-placed her at the group home. The caseworker took her to get something to eat before taking her back to the group home. By midnight we got a call that she had run away again. So of course, we were devastated. We'd been working with this girl since she was twelve.

In debriefing our decisions, I told her caseworker, 'Never underestimate the power of not using your muscle when you can. What's most important is that you build a relationship. I know you're scared for her, but she'll call you. Don't worry. The most important part of this scenario is planting the seed in the moment. We must use these moments to get the girls to understand that we care and that we are there to help and support. I know we are scared, but the reality is that if we lock her up, eventually she'll get out, and all kids have the opportunity to run.'

If a mother locks her kid in their bedroom, the kid will find a way to tunnel out! We just can't control them from running.

What we *can* control is the relationship we build with the girls. It's more important that they feel like they can call us when they need us than it is for us to flex our muscles all the time. Years ago, one of our runaway girls called us from across the country: 'Hey, I got myself into a situation. Help me get back.' She was binging on drugs and being trafficked, and had we not built that relationship, she would not have called us for help. This girl, she's still in my life right now, and she's on the road to recovery and restoration. We can't control them, and we can't control their running away. But we can build relationships. I want the girls to call me when they need me.

■ ■ ■

Again, most of the girls that we work with have been raised in foster care. They've been abused sexually and physically. They've typically been in and out of school and have moved around for most of their lives. Typically, many of them have low self-esteem, and a sexualized identity. They have little-to-no independent living skills and not much of an education. I remember when I started out, I wanted to help them get their high school diplomas and go on to college. But it's not about me. I was putting way too much on their plates. They were overwhelmed.

Now, one of my early goals is to help build a girl's self-esteem. I will take her to a career service center and help her figure out what path she might want to take. What can she do over the next six weeks? Is there a short-term certificate course that interests her? While we may want her to get from Point A to Point B, and even further down the road, let's just get her from Point A to Point A-and-a-half. Those small accomplishments will help build her self-esteem.

I'll give you a story that some people would not necessarily see as a success just yet. One of the girls in the first batch of kids I case-managed was fourteen years old when I met her.

She was in foster care because her mother had been incarcerated, and her father was not in the picture. As a youth, she'd run away from just about every placement we could find for her. She'd been sexually abused. She was emotionally attached to her trafficker. And because of the life she was living, she didn't feel like she would live beyond eighteen.

A lot of girls have talked to me about a darkness they feel when they're going to sleep. This girl felt that darkness and was tormented by voices that told her to kill herself because she wasn't worth anything. We worked really hard with her, but for years, she didn't know what to do. She was just overwhelmed.

She's now twenty-four years old, and her present goals are twofold. The first is to complete her high school diploma. The second is to get her criminal record expunged. They're all prostitution-related charges, both as a juvenile and as an adult. She is embarrassed by her past, and the way potential employers make her feel when they see her charges just makes things worse. I am assisting her with getting her record expunged, and helping her to get a better job, perhaps as a student intern. These are her baby steps. She's in a space where I consider her stable. She's looking after her little boy. She's not going back to 'the life' and has not relapsed. I count that a success story.

It may not be a success for some people on the outside. She doesn't have her diploma. She doesn't have a great job. But not relapsing is a success. We're still working on her journey, right? She's doing well—and she knows that she can still call me for help. I have other girls who call me when they need me. They call me when they're having suicidal thoughts or for something as simple as having questions about caring for a child. Many of them are still working through their trauma. They still need some help on their journey.

One way I like to help is by identifying the strengths these girls have. They are incredibly resilient, and they are so much stronger than they think they are. They're the strongest young women I've ever worked with. They've survived the hardest parts of life, and they've endured things that children should never have to endure. I just want them to know that I am here to help them on their journey to redemption.

AFTERWORD

The women in each of the chapters of this book have given us a precious gift. As they have made themselves vulnerable, these beautiful souls have courageously allowed us into a most sacred and guarded place—the depths of the human heart.

They have shared with us the sorrow, the heartbreak, the disillusion of hopeless and helpless moments in their lives. For those of us who have experienced similar narratives in our own lives, we understand and we weep with the transgressions that took place. We are honored to know of their deep pain—but more than that—it is a privilege and an inspiration to witness their glorious freedom, for each of them has found ways to overcome what for many of us seems unimaginable.

It would be close to impossible to read this book and not respond with extreme grief. It's actually okay to have felt a sense of sadness, or even loss, as you read through each chapter. It's understandable to feel shaken to your core and to even sense anger. Responding with these emotions makes us human and more like Jesus at the same time. When we perceive the injustice—and anger arises, and pain pierces our heart—we have an opportunity. This opportunity invites us to take all these responses and sift them through the love of Jesus, and when we do this, it becomes the launchpad to something that can be life-changing and revolutionary in the lives of others.

We know that the numbers of women who are assaulted and abused are higher than statistics reflect; so many incidents go unreported. Stories similar to those you have just read are taking place in your very own communities. This holy awareness, this holy heartbreak is what initiated BRAVE. The idea, the dream that we could radically reduce the number of women being trafficked, set us off on this journey to reach and connect with the most vulnerable girls in our cities. BRAVE is committed to platforming the real-life stories of real-life women in order to bring an awareness that will open the eyes of community leaders, governments, schools, pastors, and churches.

The sooner a girl knows her value, the stronger her resolve will be to make better choices. The key is informing her how marvelous she is in the sight of her Creator and in our sight as well. My co-founder, Danielle Strickland, our CEO, Miley Waterman, and I are constantly dreaming up ways to get the message out: *girls are not the problem; girls are the solution.*

The women you read about are warriors. Their victory is our triumph; their healing is our joy; their courage is our hope. Join us by continuing to pray for every one of them, as their lives display the faithful and relentless love of God. And pray for those who have yet to come into contact with a BRAVE soul who would lead them to the freedom and healing found in Jesus. He is what we most need—but we also need each other. He made us this way. He made us for community.

A couple of years ago, I spoke about BRAVE at a gathering of leaders. A woman came up to me when I finished and said to me, "I'm so glad you are reaching out to girls in foster care. I came to fall in love with Jesus as an adult, but it took me a while to forgive the church because as an adult, I wondered where the church was when I was a foster kid."

Wow!

That conversation has turned many of the excuses we hear into combustible fuel. What if every church said about exploitation, "Not on our watch . . . not in our neighborhood." So now what? Well, the invitation is open: will you be *brave* with us?

Noemi Chavez, co-founder, BRAVE Global

I AM BRAVE

Brave is not a song that everyone can sing.
It is a melody learned by the lionhearted.
It sounds like blood rushing
in your ears, while your hands are white-knuckled
looking fear in the face and saying, "Not today."

Brave feels like your lungs filling with air.
Each slow breath a revolution
because it hurts sometimes
to even breathe.
It is the inchworm that chooses to climb the biggest tree.
Some days Brave is just two feet on the floor
because you made it out of bed.

Brave pokes holes in the dark
until it becomes a starry night.
Stand in the twinkle light.
Remember you can paint your own.

Brave is, "Today my eyes did not become leaky clouds."
Or Brave says, "Today I let it rain," and it was a thunderstorm,
but even the smallest flower will eventually see the sun.

Brave looks in the mirror and does think about its thighs.
Brave says, "This is how I was made.
There are no flaws in this design."

Brave is, "Today other people's hurtful words
will be silent films.
I will see their lips moving,
but the words will have no meaning.
In a backlash of love, I will write a new script."

Brave listens to the small flame flickering inside you that says,
"Feed this unflinching fire with the kindling of kind words."
Surround yourself with friends that hold you up like balloons.

Brave is I am here for a reason.
I am the answer to someone else's prayer.
I don't have all the answers,
but nothing is going to stop me from finding out.

Brave should be on my name tag;
it should be my superhero name.
Because, let's face it. I look better with a cape.
When people ask me what is your name?
I will say:
I am Brave.
What is your superpower?

By Dagmar Morgan, used by gracious permission.

RESOURCES

Helpful Survivor and Prevention Resources

www.braveglobal.org
www.braveglobal.ca
www.celebraterecovery.com
www.endingthegame.com
www.endslaverynow.org
www.exoduscry.com
www.freedomnetworkusa.org
www.fairgirls.org
www.gemsuncovered.org
www.humantraffickinghotline.org
www.iamatreasure.com
www.polarisproject.org
www.rahabsdaughters.org
www.thecupcakegirls.org
www.unicefusa.org/mission/protect/trafficking

Global Initiatives

www.a21.org
www.stopthetraffik.org
www.gaatw.org
www.love146.org/mission-vision
www.healtrafficking.org/resources/end-child-prostitution-
and-trafficking-ecpat

Documentaries

Nefarious: Merchant of Souls, 2011 (available on YouTube)
I am Jane Doe, 2017 (available on Netflix)
Brides and Brothels: The Rohingya Trade, 2018 (available on YouTube)
'Sex Trafficking in America,' *Frontline*, Season 37, Episode 21, 2019 (available on PBS)

Books

Kevin Bales, *Disposable People: New Slavery in the Global Economy*
Kevin Bales and Ron Soodalter, *The Slave Next Door: Human Trafficking and Slavery in America Today*
Harmony Dust, *Scars and Stilettos: The Transformation of an Exotic Dancer* (iamatreasure.com/shop)
Stephanie Hepburn and Rita J. Simon, *Human Trafficking Around the World: Hidden in Plain Sight*
Rachel Lloyd, *Girls Like Us: Fighting for a World Where Girls Are Not for Sale: A Memoir*
Beth Moore, *Breaking Free: Discover the Victory of Total Surrender*
Joyce Meyer, *Beauty for Ashes: Receiving Emotional Healing*
Lewis B. Smedes, *Shame and Grace: Healing the Shame We Don't Deserve*

ACKNOWLEDGMENTS

In putting this book together, I am indebted to so many.

First, to my wife, Kerry: thank you for your deep-core faith, your deep-core joy, and your deep-core kindness. You make me want to be a better man. And thank you for your patient smiles when I say, again, "Only six or eight more hours, and I'll be done with the final edit." I know that you know it will take longer than that.

Thanks to Danielle Strickland: you bring light wherever you go, and all who meet you are better off for having done so. Thank you for the hope and the inspiration you carry. And thank you for all the encouragement as *Brave in Real Life* came to life.

Thanks to Miley Waterman: as CEO of BRAVE Global, your input and direction made this a better book.

Thanks to Stephen Court for disciplining unruly text and correcting spell-check's leniencies.

Thanks to Dagmar Morgan for graciously allowing me to include the poems she presented at the first Canadian BRAVE event in Toronto.

Thanks to Judy Artindale: you are my ideal reader.

Thanks to my editor at 100 Movements Publishing, Anna Robinson: it has been a pleasure working with you, and you've helped shape this into a beautiful book.

Lastly, thanks to Mariah, Alicia, Harmony, Tangelia, Noemi, Sharmila (Sam), Taanis, Heidi, and Terrika: your trust, your openness, and your courageous resilience inspire me.

NOTES

INTRODUCTION

[1] Malika Saada Saar, "Stopping the Foster Care to Child Trafficking Pipeline," October 29, 2013, huffpost.com/entry/stopping-the-foster-care-_b_4170483. See also, "Sex Trafficking: Sex and human trafficking in the U.S. disproportionately affects foster youth," NFYI, nfyi.org/issues/sex-trafficking/. In 2012, 58 percent of 72 sexually trafficked girls before the Los Angeles Court were foster care kids. That same year, Commercial Sexual Exploitation of Children (CSEC) estimated that between 50 to 80 percent of sexually exploited children were in or had come through the child welfare system. California Against Slavery Research and Education (CASRE).

Reported in 2016, the Commissioner of the Connecticut Department of Children and Families, the Honorable Joette Katz, stated that in Connecticut, 98 percent of children who are identified as survivors of sex trafficking had previous involvement with child welfare services. Eighty-five percent of commercially exploited children in New York State came from group homes and foster care; 75 percent from New York city. See "An Unholy Alliance: The Connection between Foster Care and Human Trafficking," Human Trafficking Search, https://humantraffickingsearch.org/wp-content/uploads/2017/09/Copy-of-An-Unholy-Alliance_The-Connection-Between-Foster-Care-and-Human-Trafficking.pdf.

In 2018, the U.S. Department of Housing and Urban Development estimated that generically, "up to 80% of children/youth who are currently or formerly under foster care become victims of sex trafficking." See "Domestic Child Sex Trafficking and Children in Foster Care," Justice Clearing House, https://justiceclearinghouse.com/resource/domestic-child-sex-trafficking-and-children-in-foster-care/.

2 Another book, *Prostitution Narratives*, is subtitled: *Stories of Survival in the Sex Trade.*

3 "World Bank Fact Sheet: Violence Against Women Worldwide," cited in Gary Haugen and Victor Boutros, *The Locust Effect: Why the End of Poverty Requires the End of Violence* (Oxford University Press, 2014) 56–57.

4 "How Empowering Girls and Women Can Change the World," Plan International, https://stories.plancanada.ca/how-empowering-girls-and-women-can-change-the-world/.

5 "National Intimate Partner and Sexual Violence Survey," 2010, 2. Invariably, the question is asked, "What about boys?" They too are subjected to abuse and exploitation. However, "nearly 1 in 5 women (18.3%) and 1 in 71 men (1.4%) in the United States have been raped at some time in their lives." The disparity speaks volumes. See https://www.cdc.gov/violenceprevention/pdf/nisvs_report2010-a.pdf.

6 Haugen and Boutros, *The Locust Effect,* 56–7.

7 "Human Trafficking by the Numbers," Human Rights First, January 7, 2017, https://www.humanrightsfirst.org/resource/human-trafficking-numbers.

8 Jaclyn Gallucci, "Human Trafficking Is an Epidemic in the U.S. It's Also Big Business," *Fortune*, April 14, 2019, https://fortune.com/2019/04/14/human-sex-trafficking-us-slavery/.

9 https://edge.ca/news/4186737/human-trafficking-survivor-story/, May 4, 2018.

10 "Human Trafficking in Canada, Ontario, and Peel," Peel Institute on Violence Prevention, Family Services of Peel, February 2018, https://fspeel.org/wp-content/uploads/2018/04/Human_Trafficking_in_Canada_Ontario_and_Peel_Feb2018.pdf.

11 International Justice Mission (IJM) is a global human rights agency that aims to end slavery for good by partnering with local law enforcement and justice systems.

12 Haugen and Boutros, *The Locust Effect*, 233.

1 O ROMEO, ROMEO! WHEREFORE ART THOU ROMEO?

1 Quoted in Jody Raphael, *Listening to Olivia: Violence, Poverty, and Prostitution* (Northeastern University Press, 2004), 46.

2 Nicole A. Barrett, "An Assessment of Sex Trafficking," *Global Justice Associates*, May 2013, commissioned by Canadian Women's Foundation—Task Force on Trafficking of Women and Girls in Canada, 14, https://www.canadiancentretoendhumantrafficking.ca/wp-content/uploads/2016/10/Assessment-of-Sex-Trafficking-in-Canada.pdf.

3 Cited in Benjamin Perrin, *Invisible Chains: Canada's Underground World Of Human Trafficking* (Viking, 2010), 115.

4 Elisa Cloutier, "La prostitution juvénile en forte demande à Québec," *Le Journal de Quebec,* February 27, 2019.

5 Nisha Lilia Diu, "Welcome to Paradise: Inside the world of legalised prostitution," *Telegraph,* January 28, 2015, 12, https://s.telegraph.co.uk/graphics/projects/welcome-to-paradise/. Casandra Diamond, "How I was recruited into sex trafficking," *Toronto Star,* October 21, 2019, E1, https://www.thestar.com/life/health_wellness/2019/10/21/how-i-was-recruited-into-sex-trafficking.html.

6 Seema Marwaha, "'Anyone can be a victim': Canadian high school girls being lured into sex trade," *CBC NEWS,* January 29, 2017, https://www.cbc.ca/amp/1.3956214. This news article cited local police estimates at $280,000 annually.

7 Perrin, *Invisible Chains,* 111.

8 Telephone interview with Sergeant Brad Brooker, June 13, 2019, used by permission.

9 William Shakespeare, *Romeo and Juliet*, Act III, Scene 1, Lines 61–2, from "The Folger Shakespeare," Barbara Mowat, Paul Werstine, Michael Poston, and Rebecca Niles, eds., *Folger Shakespeare Library*, January 18, 2021, https://shakespeare.folger.edu/shakespeares-works/romeo-and-juliet/.

10 His name has been changed.

[11] His name has been changed.

[12] His name has been changed.

[13] Gems Uncovered is an organization that seeks to rebuild the lives of those affected by sexual exploitation. www.gemsuncovered.org.

2 IT'S EASIER TO COMPLY THAN TO FIGHT

[1] Cited in Rachel Moran, *Paid For: My Journey Through Prostitution* (W. W. Norton & Company, 2015), 43.

[2] Ibid.

[3] Casandra Diamond, "How I was recruited into sex trafficking," *Toronto Star,* October 21, 2019.

[4] Her name has been changed.

[5] A case of twenty-four or thirty-six beers.

3 YOU KNOW HOW MEN ARE

[1] Alexis Okeowo, "The Fragile Existence of Sex Workers During the Pandemic," *The New Yorker*, May 21, 2020, https://www.newyorker.com/news/news-desk/the-fragile-existence-of-sex-workers-during-the-pandemic.

[2] Jess, "Ending Human Trafficking: The Link between Strip Clubs and Sexual Exploitation – closer than you think!" *Trafficking Justice Blog*, January 8, 2018, https://traffickingjusticeblog.wordpress.com/2018/01/18/ending-human-trafficking-the-link-between-strip-clubs-and-sexual-exploitation-closer-than-you-think/.

[3] Raphael, *Listening to Olivia*, 60.

[4] Jess, "Ending Human Trafficking."

[5] Sydney Loney, "This Woman Was Trafficked at a Club When She Was 19—And It Could Happen to *Anyone*," *Flare*, December 27, 2018, https://www.flare.com/news/reality-of-human-trafficking/.

[6] United Nations Office on Drugs and Crime, "UNODC on trafficking in persons and smuggling of migrants," https://www.unodc.org/unodc/en/human-trafficking/index.html.

[7] Her name has been changed.

[8] See John 15:5.

4 THEY DON'T CARE ABOUT YOU

[1] California Child Welfare Council, "An Unholy Alliance," 5.

[2] Ibid., 6.

[3] Cited in Jeffrey Reiman, *The Rich Get Richer and the Poor Get Prison: Ideology, Class, and Criminal Justice* (Allyn & Bacon, 2007), 121.

[4] The Editors, "Race and the War on Drugs," *America: The Jesuit Review*, October 22, 2007, https://www.americamagazine.org/issue/630/editorial/race-and-war-drugs.

[5] Report to the Chairman, Subcommittee on Human Resources, Committee on Ways and Means House of Representatives, April 1994, "FOSTER CARE: Parental Drug Abuse Has Alarming Impact on Young Children," https://www.gao.gov/products/HEHS-94-89.

[6] Chirp is a Nextel function that allows two phones to be used like walkie-talkies.

[7] Emergency Medical Services.

5 A BETTER LIFE IN AMERICA?

[1] Haugen and Boutros, *The Locust Effect*, 17, 44.

[2] Martin Brunt, "Essex lorry deaths: Bodies of migrants 'were so tightly packed they couldn't be checked for signs of life', court hears," *Sky News*, October 28, 2020, https://news.sky.com/story/essex-lorry-deaths-bodies-of-migrants-were-so-tightly-packed-they-couldnt-be-checked-for-signs-of-life-court-hears-12116929.

[3] "Essex lorry deaths: Victims 'tried to break through roof,'" *BBC News*, October 9, 2020, https://www.bbc.co.uk/news/uk-england-essex-54479154.

6 THIS IS ALL I'M GOOD FOR

[1] Cited in Moran, *Paid For*, 127.

[2] Ibid.

[3] Beth Moore, *Breaking Free: Discover the Victory of Total Surrender* (B&H Books, 2007).

[4] Rachel Thomas, www.endingthegame.com.

7 AN EXPERIMENT GONE WRONG

1   Andrea Dworkin, *Life and Death* (Free Press, 1997), 143.

2   Edward C. Kimelman, "No Quiet Place/ Review Committee on Indian and Metis Adoptions and Placements," 1985, Winnipeg, Manitoba Community Services, https://legislativelibrary.mb.catalogue.libraries.coop/eg/opac/record/107410115.

3   Raven Sinclair, "Identity Lost and Found: Lessons From the Sixties Scoop," *First Peoples Child and Family Review*, 2007, 66, cited in Wikipedia, "Sixties Scoop," https://en.wikipedia.org/wiki/Sixties_Scoop.

4   Paula Newton, "Canada's stolen daughters: Sex traffickers target indigenous Canadians," *CNN*, February 23, 2017. Sourced in https://fspeel.org/wp-content/uploads/2018/04/Human_Trafficking_in_Canada_Ontario_and_Peel_Feb2018.pdf.

5   Brown v. Canada (Attorney General), [2017] ONSC 251 at para. 7.

6   The Cree peoples are the largest group of First Nations in Canada. The majority of them live north and west of Lake Superior. The Blackfeet Nation traditionally lived in southern Alberta and Saskatchewan, and northern Montana. Roughly one third of First Nations people live on Reserve—land that was set apart under the Indian Act of 1876.

7   Pickton confessed to an undercover RCMP agent that he had murdered forty-nine women, and had hoped to kill one more to make it an even fifty. See Allan Dowd, "Canadian prosecutors say Pickton wanted to kill 50," *Reuters*, January 22, 2007, https://www.reuters.com/article/us-killings/canadian-prosecutors-say-pickton-wanted-to-kill-50-idUSN2240655620070122.

8 STICKERS ONLY STICK WHEN YOU LET THEM

1   Anne Lamott, *Traveling Mercies: Some Thoughts on Faith* (Anchor, 1999), 134.

2   Lewis B. Smedes, *Shame and Grace: Healing the Shame We Don't Deserve* (HarperOne, 1994), 135–6.

3   Desmond Tutu, *No Future Without Forgiveness* (Image, 1999).

4   Max Lucado, *You Are Special* (Crossway, 1997).

5   Matthew 6:12 (NLT).

6   United Service Organization.

9 BABY STEPS

1   Raphael, *Listening to Olivia*, 161, 159.

2   For more information on the Stages of Change, see https://sphweb. bumc.bu.edu/otlt/mph-modules/sb/behavioralchangetheories/ behavioralchangetheories6.html.